TIMESAVER

# Grammar

ACTIVITIES (ELEMENTARY)

## Teacher's reference key

A small clock on each page tells you approximately how long each activity should take.

Small icons at the top of each page show whether the activity is best suited to individual, pair or group work.

Individual

Pair

Group

TIMESAVER

# Grammar

ACTIVITIES (ELEMENTARY)

## Contents



 

# Have You Got The Basketball?

### How to play

- The game is for 3 players.
- Cut out the cards.
- Put the cards on the table and look at them for 5 minutes.
- Mix the cards up.
- The players start with 4 cards each. Put the other 8 cards in a pile face-down on the table.
- Ask questions and pick up cards to find pairs from one of the sets: *Clothes, Furniture, Sports, Transport* or *Food*. The winner is the player with the most pairs of cards.

### Rules

- Look at your cards. You've got to find more cards from one of the sets.
- Player 1 picks up a card from the pile.
- If Player 1 has got a pair of cards, he puts the pair face-up on the table.
- Player 1 has got, for example, the *sofa* card (a *Furniture* card), Player 1 asks Player 2 or Player 3 for another Furniture card, for example, **John, have you got the table card?** Player 1 can only ask one player.
- If Player 2 or Player 3 has got the table card, Player 1 takes the card and puts the pair of cards (the *table* card and the *sofa* card ) face-up on the table. Then it is Player 2's turn.
- If Player 2 or Player 3 hasn't got the *table* card, the turn passes to Player 2.

## Clothes cards

**jumper**

**shirt**

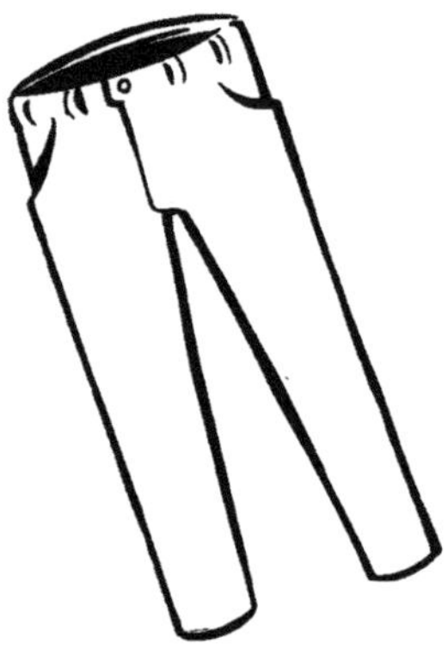

**trousers**

**gloves**

## Furniture cards

**bed**

**chair**

**sofa**

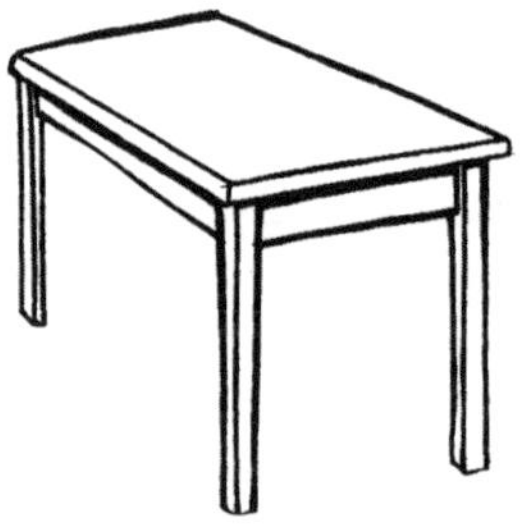

**table**

 

## Sports cards

**tennis racket**

**skis**

**basketball**

**football**

## Transport cards

**bicycle**

**motorbike**

**car**

**bus**

## Food cards

**sandwich**

**banana**

**crisps**

**chocolate**

# English Families

**Play this game in small groups.**

### How to play English Families

- Cut out the cards.
- Mix the cards up.
- Put the cards in a pile face-down on the table.
- Each player starts with 4 cards.
- Ask questions and collect sets of English family cards.

### Rules

- Collect a complete family by asking questions, for example, **Have you got Mr Smith?**
- If another player has got that card, the player answers **Yes, I have,** and gives the card to the first player.
- If no players have got that card, the first player takes the card at the top of the pile and it's the next player's turn.
- When a player has got a full family set (the mother, father, sister and brother), the player puts the set down and takes another turn.
- The winner is the player with the most English families!

**Mr Smith**
Mr Smith
Mrs Smith
Sara Smith
Sam Smith

**Mrs Smith**
Mr Smith
Mrs Smith
Sara Smith
Sam Smith

**Sara Smith**
Mr Smith
Mrs Smith
Sara Smith
Sam Smith

**Sam Smith**
Mr Smith
Mrs Smith
Sara Smith
Sam Smith

**Mr Vine**
Mr Vine
Mrs Vine
Vicky Vine
Victor Vine

**Mrs Vine**
Mr Vine
Mrs Vine
Vicky Vine
Victor Vine

**Vicky Vine**
Mr Vine
Mrs Vine
Vicky Vine
Victor Vine

**Victor Vine**
Mr Vine
Mrs Vine
Vicky Vine
Victor Vine

**Mr Chapman**

Mr Chapman
Mrs Chapman
Cherie Chapman
Charles Chapman

**Mrs Chapman**

Mr Chapman
Mrs Chapman
Cherie Chapman
Charles Chapman

**Cherie Chapman**

Mr Chapman
Mrs Chapman
Cherie Chapman
Charles Chapman

**Charles Chapman**

Mr Chapman
Mrs Chapman
Cherie Chapman
Charles Chapman

**Mr Sherman**

Mr Sherman
Mrs Sherman
Shelly Sherman
Sean Sherman

**Mrs Sherman**

Mr Sherman
Mrs Sherman
Shelly Sherman
Sean Sherman

**Shelly Sherman**

Mr Sherman
Mrs Sherman
Shelly Sherman
Sean Sherman

**Sean Sherman**

Mr Sherman
Mrs Sherman
Shelly Sherman
Sean Sherman

**Mr Hurst**

Mr Hurst
Mrs Hurst
Heather Hurst
Harry Hurst

**Mrs Hurst**

Mr Hurst
Mrs Hurst
Heather Hurst
Harry Hurst

**Heather Hurst**

Mr Hurst
Mrs Hurst
Heather Hurst
Harry Hurst

**Harry Hurst**

Mr Hurst
Mrs Hurst
Heather Hurst
Harry Hurst

**Mr Richards**
Mr Richards
Mrs Richards
Rosa Richards
Ricky Richards

**Mrs Richards**
Mr Richards
Mrs Richards
Rosa Richards
Ricky Richards

**Rosa Richards**
Mr Richards
Mrs Richards
Rosa Richards
Ricky Richards

**Ricky Richards**
Mr Richards
Mrs Richards
Rosa Richards
Ricky Richards

**Mr Lawson**
Mr Lawson
Mrs Lawson
Louise Lawson
Liam Lawson

**Mrs Lawson**
Mr Lawson
Mrs Lawson
Louise Lawson
Liam Lawson

**Louise Lawson**
Mr Lawson
Mrs Lawson
Louise Lawson
Liam Lawson

**Liam Lawson**
Mr Lawson
Mrs Lawson
Louise Lawson
Liam Lawson

**Mr West**
Mr West
Mrs West
Wendy West
William West

**Mrs West**
Mr West
Mrs West
Wendy West
William West

**Wendy West**
Mr West
Mrs West
Wendy West
William West

**William West**
Mr West
Mrs West Wendy
West William West

 

# Wild Animals in North America

**Complete the texts. Write the verbs using the correct form of the present simple.**

**Match texts 1 – 3 with the pictures A – C.**

**Example:** A lot of wild animals **live** (*live*) in north America.

**1** Raccoons (1) ________________ (*come*) from the forests of north America. The mother raccoon (2) ________________ (*have*) four, five or six babies in spring. The babies (3) ________________ (*not / can*) see anything for about three weeks. They (4) ________________ (*stay*) with their parents for the first year.

**2** The skunk also (5) ________________ (*live)* in north America. The skunk (6) ________________ (*have got*) a bad smell and it (7) ________________ (*use*) the smell to fight other animals and people. The skunk's smell (8) ________________ (*not / go away*) easily or quickly! Skunks (9) ________________ (*eat*) insects and other small animals.

**3** Coyotes (10) ________________ (*look*) like wolves, but they (11) ________________ (be) different. Wolves usually (12) ________________ (*stay*) with other wolves, but coyotes (13) ________________ (*not like*) company: they (14) ________________ (*prefer*) to be alone. Coyotes (15) ________________ (*be*) intelligent. They (16)________________ (*eat*) a lot of different animals, and their favourite food is rabbits. South Dakota (17) ________________ (*be*) the Coyote State! Did you know that?

**Match texts 1 – 3 with the pictures A – C.**

**A**

☐

**B**

☐

**C**

☐

# The Pet Game

### How to play

- The game is for 2– 4 players.
- Cut out the numbers and put them in a bag or an envelope.
- In turns, players take a number from the bag and read the sentence in the game with that number.
- The sentences are all **wrong** and the player has got to make the sentences negative. Use *isn't, aren't, don't, doesn't* or *can't*.
- If the player says the sentence correctly, he/she keeps the number.
- If the player is wrong, he/she puts the number back in the bag.
- The player with the most numbers at the end of the game wins.

| | | |
|---|---|---|
| **1** A mouse is a very large pet. | **2** Cats drink lemonade. | **3** Tortoises are more playful than dogs. |
| **4** A tortoise can run very fast. | **5** A hamster eats eggs. | **6** Birds sing at night. |
| **7** People take their cats for walks. | **8** Cats can speak English. | **9** Dogs can fly. |
| **10** Snakes play with dogs. | **11** Snakes can hop. | **12** Fish are noisy pets. |
| **13** Spiders eat dogs. | **14** Horses eat meat. | **15** Rabbits can swim. |
| **16** Pets always sleep in the house. | **17** Dogs wear a coat in winter. | **18** A pet goes to hospital to have a baby. |

| | | | | | | | | |
|---|---|---|---|---|---|---|---|---|
| 1 | 2 | 3 | 4 | 5 | 6 | 7 | 8 | 9 |
| 10 | 11 | 12 | 13 | 14 | 15 | 16 | 17 | 18 |

 

# After School

**What do these children do after school?**

**1** **Match the children with the activities. Then complete the sentences.**

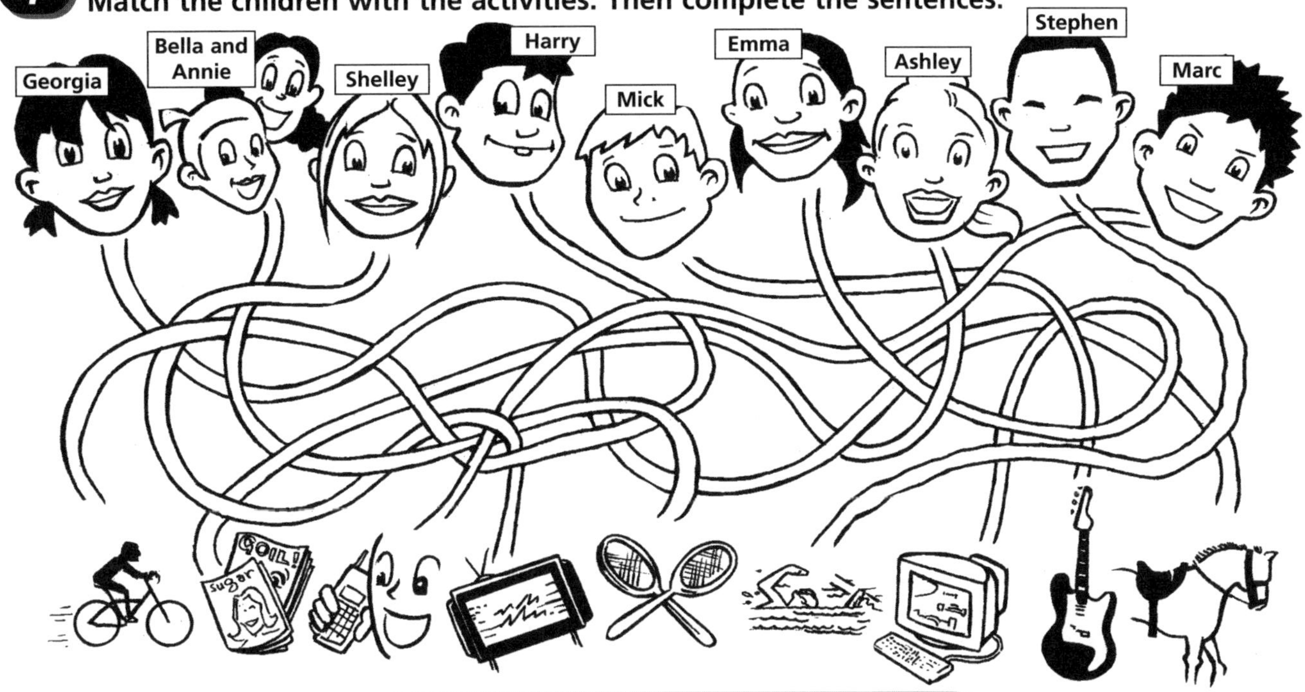


**Example:** Georgia *goes horse-riding*.

**1** Bella and Annie ______

**2** Shelley ______

**3** Harry ______

**4** Mick ______

**5** Emma ______

**6** Ashley ______

**7** Stephen ______

**8** Marc ______ his friends.

**2** **Write sentences about what you do after school. Choose from the pictures in exercise 1, or invent your own sentences. Then compare your sentences with a partner.**

______

______

# Getting To Know Someone

**1** **Complete the questions with the correct form of *be* or *do*.**

**2** **Now write your answers below each question.**

**3** **Give your completed paper to your teacher. Your teacher will give you another student's sheet. Read the answers. Ask your classmates to find out whose paper it is.**

| | |
|---|---|
| **1** Are you a boy or a girl?<br>------------------------------ | **2** What type of music ______ you like?<br>------------------------------ |
| **3** How old ______ you?<br>------------------------------ | **4** ______ you good at maths?<br>------------------------------ |
| **5** ______ your father drive a car?<br>------------------------------ | **6** ______ you good at drawing?<br>------------------------------ |
| **7** ______ you know any famous people?<br>------------------------------ | **8** ______ you good at sport?<br>------------------------------ |
| **9** ______ you play tennis?<br>------------------------------ | **10** ______ you live in a house or a flat?<br>------------------------------ |
| **11** ______ you tall?<br>------------------------------ | **12** ______ your grandparents live with you?<br>------------------------------ |
| **13** ______ your best friend older than you?<br>------------------------------ | **14** ______ you ever visit other countries on holiday?<br>------------------------------ |
| **15** ______ you play a musical instrument?<br>------------------------------ | **16** ______ you walk to school?<br>------------------------------ |
| **17** ______ your surname more than seven letters long?<br>------------------------------ | **18** ______ your eyes blue?<br>------------------------------ |
| **19** ______ you like horror films?<br>------------------------------ | **20** How many languages ______ you speak?<br>------------------------------ |

 

# In Britain

**Chantal and Colette are on holiday in Britain.**

**Look at the pictures and write the answers to the questions.**
**Use the expressions in the box.**

| | | | |
|---|---|---|---|
| No, you don't. | Yes, we have. | Yes, I am. | Yes, you are. |
| No, we haven't. | ~~Yes, you do.~~ | | |

# Get Fit!

**Look at the pictures of what Billy usually does in a typical week. Then look at the pictures of what Billy is doing this week. Write sentences to compare a typical week with this week.**

## Billy's typical week

**Monday**

**Tuesday**

**Wednesday**

**Thursday**

**Friday**

**Saturday**

**Sunday**

## This week

**Monday**

**Tuesday**

**Wednesday**

**Thursday**

**Friday**

**Saturday**

**Sunday**

**Example:** Billy usually watches TV after school on Mondays. Today, he's working out in the gym.

**1** What does Billy usually eat for breakfast on Tuesdays? What is he eating today?

He usually ----------------------------------------------

Today, he ----------------------------------------------

**2** What does Billy usually do after school on Wednesdays? What is he doing today?

He usually ----------------------------------------------

Today, he ----------------------------------------------

**3** What does Billy usually have for lunch on Thursdays? What is he having today?

He usually ----------------------------------------------

Today, he ----------------------------------------------

**4** What does Billy usually do during breaktime on Fridays? What is he doing today?

He usually ----------------------------------------------

Today, he ----------------------------------------------

**5** What does Billy usually read on Saturdays? What is he doing today?

He usually ----------------------------------------------

Today, he ----------------------------------------------

**6** What does Billy usually do on Sunday afternoons? What is he doing today?

He usually ----------------------------------------------

Today, he ----------------------------------------------

 

# Our World

**Play this game in small groups. You need: 1 coin and 1 counter for each player. One person, who doesn't play, is the referee. The referee has the Answer Key.**

**How to play Our World**
- Toss the coin.
- Move 1 space if you get 'heads'.
- Move 2 spaces if you get 'tails'.

**Scoring**
- For every correct answer, you get the points in that square.
- For every wrong answer, you lose the points in that square.
- The winner is the player who finishes with the most points.

**START**

**1** You d_________ when you're thirsty. (3)

**2** Planes m_________ a lot of noise. (2)

**3** A chef c_________ food. (1)

**4** People g_________ u_________ in the mornings. (1)

**8** Cows e_________ grass. (1)

**7** Coffee c_________ from south America. (2)

**6** People l_________ if something is funny. (3)

**5** A musician p_________ an instrument. (2)

**9** Rain f_________ from the sky. (2)

**10** Birds h_________ g____ wings. (3)

**11** Bats s_________ during the day. (3)

**12** People w_________ on two legs. (1)

**16** Birds b_________ nests. (1)

**15** Many birds f_________ south in winter. (2)

**14** A baby c_________ when it is hungry. (2)

**13** A flower g_________ from a seed. (3)

**17** Fish l_________ in water. (3)

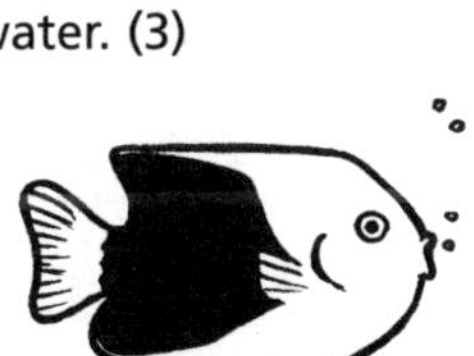

**18** Wild animals h_________ for food. (2)

**19** The moon s_________ at night. (3)

**20** Cyclists r_________ bicycles. (1)

**FINISH**

**REFEREE'S ANSWER KEY**
**1** drink **2** make **3** cooks **4** get up **5** plays **6** laugh **7** comes **8** eat **9** falls **10** have got **11** sleep **12** walk
**13** grows **14** cries **15** fly **16** build **17** live **18** hunt **19** shines **20** ride

# Bananas in Pyjamas

**1** **Match the verbs with the pictures.**

**brush**
**dip**
**sprinkle**
**roll up**

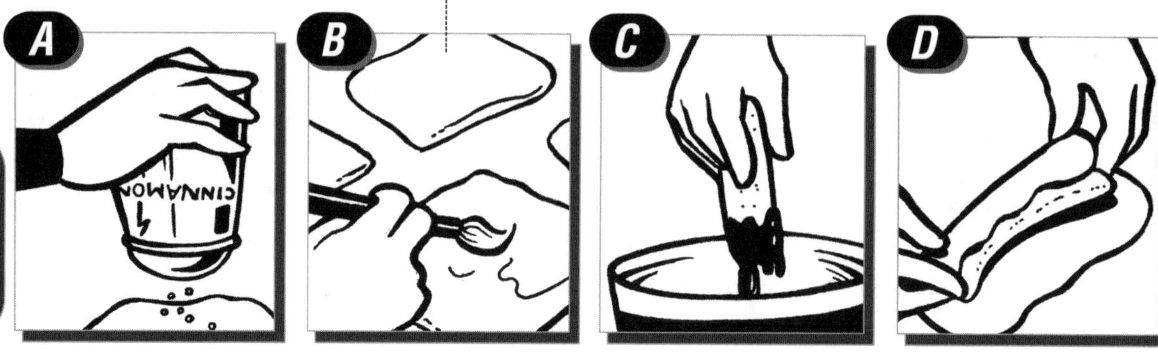

**2** **Read the dessert recipe. The recipe texts aren't in the correct order, but the pictures are in the correct order. Match the recipe instructions with the pictures.**

**A** Dip the ends of the bananas into the melted chocolate. ___
**B** Roll out the pastry. 1
**C** Put the bananas into an oven at 200°C. ___
**D** Sprinkle some cinnamon onto the pastry. ___
**E** Put the bananas on a baking tray. ___
**F** Take them out of the oven after 15 minutes. ___
**G** Brush the pastry with some egg. ___
**H** Roll up the banana in the pastry. ___
**I** Cut the pastry. ___
**J** Sprinkle some sugar onto the pastry. ___
**K** Wait until they are cool – about half an hour. ___
**L** Brush the rolled pastry with more egg. ___

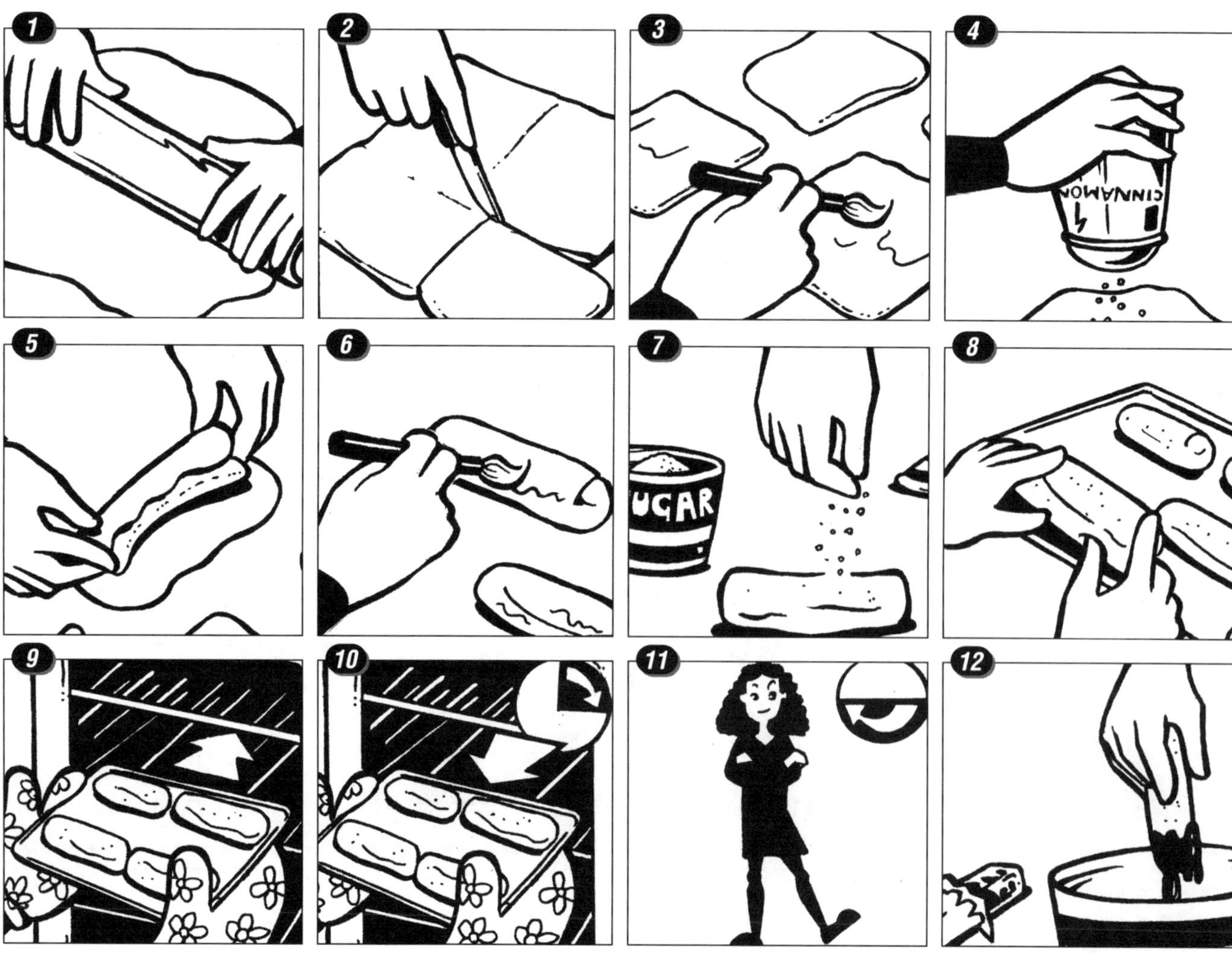

 

# When I Grow Up

**What is Charles going to be when he grows up?**

**1** Unscramble the words and put them in the sentences.

**A** brsibat **B** snoic **C** aimcg **D** scrad **E** veern

A I'm going to pull ☐◯☐☐◯☐☐ from hats.

B I'm going to take ☐☐◯☐☐ out of children's ears.

C I'm going to use ◯☐◯☐☐ .

D I'm going to use playing ◯◯☐☐☐ .

E I'm ◯☐☐☐☐ going to tell you how I do it!

**2** Now write down the letters from inside the circles above.
Unscramble the letters to find out what Charles is going to be.

◯◯◯◯◯◯◯◯

**3** What are they going to be when they grow up? Complete the sentences.

**artist teacher pilot ~~vet~~ musician comedian**

I want to look after animals.

I want to travel around the world.

I want to help children to read and write.

I want to make people laugh.

**1** He's going to be a vet **2** He ______ **3** He ______ **4** She ______

I want to paint pictures.

I want to sing and play the guitar.

**5** She ______ **6** She ______

**What are you going to be when you grow up?**

______

# The Crystal Ball

A fortune-teller is going to visit your class today.
She's going to tell you about your future. What will she say?

**Write the names of students in your class.**
**Write one name each for 1–6 and two names each for 7–12.**
**In groups, compare your answers.**

**Example: A: I think that Sara and Danny will be actors.**
**B: Yes, I think that Sara will be an actor, but not Danny. I think that you will be an actor!**

**One student will...**

1 be a doctor

................................................

2 have five children

................................................

3 marry a famous person

................................................

4 visit many countries

................................................

5 sing on TV

................................................

6 make a lot of money

................................................

**Two students will...**

7 be actors

........................ ........................

8 live in the UK

........................ ........................

9 write a lot of books

........................ ........................

10 live for 100 years

........................ ........................

11 play for a famous football team

........................ ........................

12 go to the moon

........................ ........................

 

# The Future Is In Your Hands!

**Complete the sentences with *will* or *won't*. In pairs, compare your answers.**

## ABOUT ME

**1** My best friend ________ have three children.
**2** I ________ go to Disneyland, Paris.
**3** I ________ drive a Rolls Royce car.
**4** My friends ________ give me a big 18th birthday party.
**5** My family ________ live in a big house.
**6** I ________ study at university.
**7** I ________ live abroad.
**8** I ________ run a marathon.

## ABOUT THE WORLD

**1** TVs ________ be inside watches.
**2** We ________ visit other planets.
**3** People ________ have more free time than now.
**4** People ________ do all their shopping on the Internet.
**5** People ________ live for 150 years or more.
**6** Most people ________ work from home.
**7** Doctors ________ find a cure for AIDS.
**8** All school lessons ________ be on computers.

# What Time...?

**What time do the things happen?**

## 1 Complete the dialogues.

● **John:** I'll miss you, darling. What time **does** your plane **arrive** (arrive) in Barcelona?

**Laura:** Well, I (1) ________ (check in) at the airport one hour before the flight. My plane (2) ________ (take off) at seven o'clock, so I (3) ________ (arrive) in Barcelona at ten o'clock.

● **Ian:** Excuse me, what time (4) ________ the next train to Newcastle ________ (leave)?

**Guard:** Well, there are three trains. The first is a slow train and it (5) ________ (depart) at four thirty. Then there are two fast trains that (6) ________ (leave) at five o'clock. One train (7) ________ (go) via York and the other (8) ________ (stop) at Coventry and Preston. You (9) ________ (change) at Preston for Newcastle.

● **Alice:** Mum, when (10) ________ Alex ________ (get) to Grandma's?

**Mum:** Well, his train (11) ________ (take) two hours. The taxi (12) ________ (collect) him at the station, so they (13) ________ (arrive) at Grandma's at about six thirty.

● **Gary:** What?! What time (14) ________ the film ________ (start)? OK, and what time (15) ________ the doors ________ (open)?

## 2 Match the dialogues with the people in the picture.

A **Guard**

B ________

C ________

D ________

E ________

F ________

G ________

 

# The Marie Celeste

**1** Read the story about the Marie Celeste and fill in the gaps with *was* or *were*.

The Marie Celeste (1) ________ a ship. On 5 December 1872, the Marie Celeste (2) ________ in the middle of the Atlantic Ocean. There (3) ________ something strange about this ship, so the captain of another ship, the Dei Gratia, stopped his ship and went on board the Marie Celeste with another man. They (4) ________ surprised because there (5) ________ no people on the ship at all. It (6) ________ completely empty.

There (7) ________ a lot of food on the ship. And in the kitchen, there (8) ________ saucepans of food, half cooked – but the fire (9) ________ out. In the captain's room, there (10) ________ some half-finished breakfast on the table: there (11) ________ an egg and an open bottle of medicine. Everything (12) ________ in its place. The men (13) ________ not there, but all of their clothes and things (14) ________ there. Did the men jump off the ship? But why?

The captain of the Dei Gratia looked at the book on the table. The last date in it (15) ________ 25 November. Did the men leave after that day? (16) ________ the Marie Celeste in the Atlantic without men for ten days? People wanted to know. So, they looked for information and found that it (17) ________ an American ship. It left New York with ten people on it: Captain Briggs, seven crewmen, the captain's wife and young daughter. No one saw them again and no one knows what happened to them.

**2** Here is a picture of the Marie Celeste when the captain of the Dei Gratia went aboard.
Circle the wrong things in the picture. Why are they wrong?

# Cookery Crossword

**Yesterday Katie cooked an egg dish for breakfast for her family.**

**1** **Complete the sentences. Use the past simple form of the verbs in the box.**

**add cook enjoy lift mix ~~pour~~ sprinkle turn**

**1**

She **poured** some milk into the bowl with the eggs.

**2**

She ______________ the milk and the eggs together.

**3**

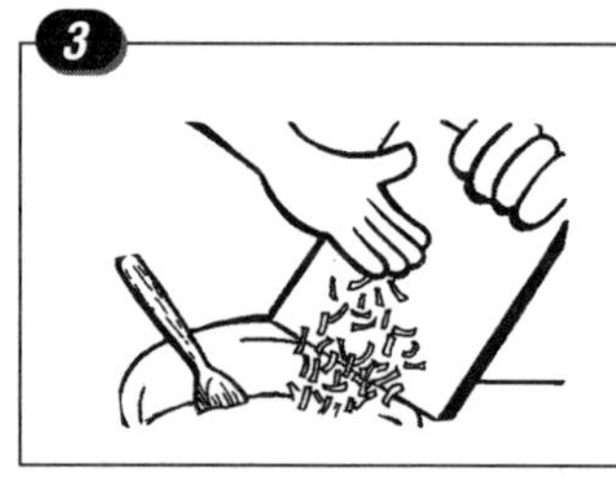

Then she ______________ some grated cheese to the mixture.

**4**

Finally, she ______________ some salt and pepper into the mixture.

**5**

She ______________ the mixture in a frying pan.

**6**

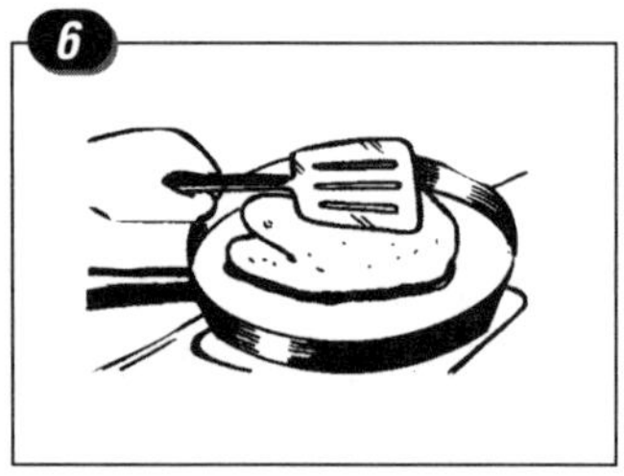

When it was cooked, she ______________ one half over the other.

**7**

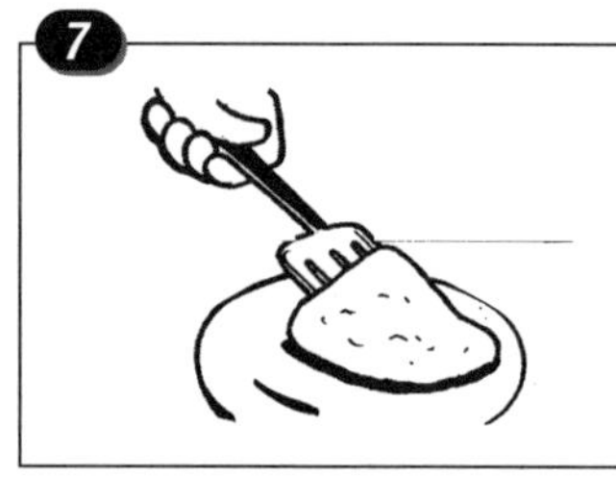

She ______________ it onto a plate carefully.

**8**

Everyone ______________ their breakfast!

**2** **Complete the puzzle with the verbs from exercise**

| | | | | | | | | | | | | |
|---|---|---|---|---|---|---|---|---|---|---|---|---|
| 1 | | | | | | P | O | U | R | E | D | |
| 2 | | | | | | | | | | | | |
| 3 | | | | A | | | | | | | | |
| 4 | S | | | | | | | | | | | |
| 5 | | | C | | | | | | | | | |
| 6 | | | | | | | T | | | | | |
| 7 | | | | L | | | | | | | | |
| 8 | | E | | | | | | | | | | |

**3** **What did Katie cook for her family? Write the letters from inside the circles above to find the name of the dish.**

Katie cooked an O _ _ _ _ _ _ _ for her family.

 

# Story Puzzle

**What happened in the story?**

**1 Complete the crossword. Use the past simple affirmative form of the verbs in the box.**

**ask carry cry drop dry jump pay play ~~stop~~ use**

## DOWN

**1** The taxi *stopped* next to us.
**3** Mum ____________ my sister's eyes with a tissue. 'OK, let's go to the park,' said Mum.
**5** Mum ____________ the driver £6.80. Then we ran into the park.
**7** Mum ____________ her umbrella to get the money.
**8** My little sister ____________ because she wanted to play in the park.

## ACROSS

**2** I ____________ in the park with my sister for an hour.
**4** 'Mum, you ____________ some money. It's under the driver's seat!' I said.
**6** My little sister and I ____________ into the taxi.
**9** Then I ____________ my sister home because Mum hadn't got any more money for a taxi!
**10** 'Why are you crying again?' I ____________ her.

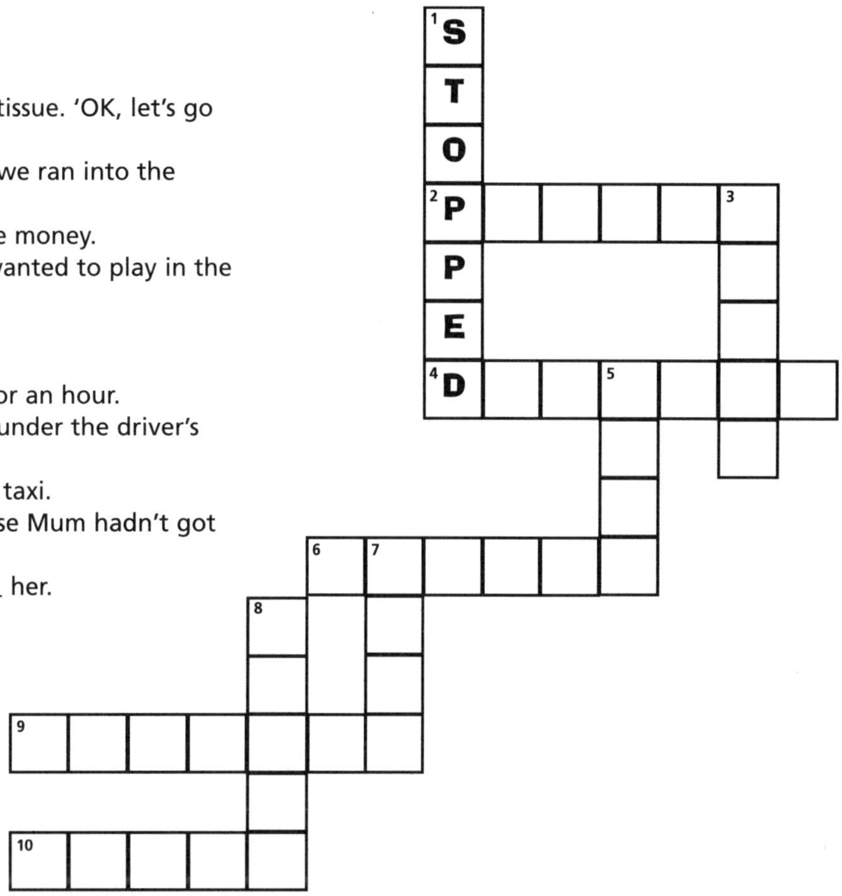


**2 Now look at the pictures. Write the story in the correct order.**

**Example: My little sister cried because she wanted to play in the park. 'Why are you crying again?' I asked her.**

# Yesterday At the Fair

**Yesterday, Jessica went to the fair.**

**1** Match the pictures on the left with the sentences on the right.

A

B

C

D
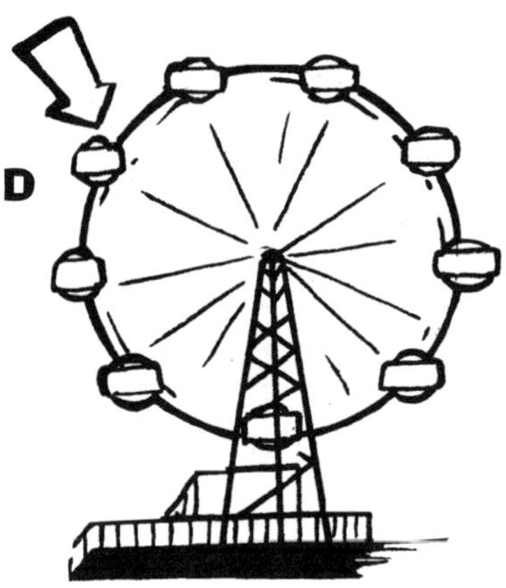

E

F

**She ate a candy floss.**

**She bought two balloons.**

**She drank a can of Cola.**

**She went on the big wheel twice.**

**She went on the rollercoaster three times.**

**She had one go at throwing the ring and won a teddy bear.**

**2** How much money did Jessica spend at the fair?

| | | | |
|---|---|---|---|
| **Throw the ring £1 = 3 rings** | **Balloons 80p** | **Cola 60p** | **Big Wheel £3.00** |
| | **Candy Floss 75p** | **Rollercoaster £4.00** | |

 

# The Hare and the Tortoise

**Read the story about the race between the hare and the tortoise.**
**Who do think will win the race?**

**Complete the story with the past simple form of the verbs.**

One day the hare and the tortoise decided to have a race. The hare **knew** that he (1) ________ (can) run faster than the tortoise. But the tortoise (2) ________ (be) more intelligent than the hare.

'Yes, I'll race you,' (3) ________ (say) the clever tortoise.

The tortoise (4) ________ (have) a clever plan. He (5) ________ (find) his brothers and sisters and he (6) ________ (tell) them to wait in different places along the path of the race. So they all (7) ________ (hide) behind the trees along the path.

The race (8) ________ (begin)! The tortoise (9) ________ (run) as fast as possible. But the hare (10) ________ (be) faster, of course.

'This will be a very easy race,' (11) ________ (think) the hare. So the hare decided to have a rest, and he quickly (12) ________ (fall) asleep at the side of the road.

Suddenly, the hare (13) ________ (wake up) and he (14) ________ (see) a tortoise ahead of him! 'How did he get ahead of me?' the hare asked himself. In fact, it (15) ________ (not be) his friend the tortoise: it (16) ________ (be) the tortoise's sister. But to a hare, all tortoises look the same.

The hare (17) ________ (run) past the tortoise easily. Soon, he (18) ________ (can't) see the tortoise, so he (19) ________ (sit) down and (20) ________ (have) another rest.

Then the hare (21) ________ (get up) and continued the race. But – as the hare happily (22) ________ (come) around the last corner before the finish line – his friend the tortoise crossed the line and (23) ________ (win) the race!

# The Fishing Trip

**Tim and Karl are brothers. The two brothers went fishing yesterday. What happened?**

**1 Complete the sentences with the past simple form of the verbs.**

1 Yesterday, my brother and I **went** (go) fishing.

2 I ______ (catch) a very big fish and my brother ______ (help) me to pull it into the boat.

3 But, when we ______ (try) to take the fish out of the water, our boat ______ (turn) over!

4 The fish ______ (swim) away, but I ______ (hold) onto the line.

5 The fish ______ (take) me to his friends – some sharks!

6 So I ______ (say) goodbye to the fish very quickly and ______ (leave) as fast as I ______ (can)!

**2 Match the sentences with the pictures.**

A

B

C

D

E

F

**3 Compare your answers with your partner. Did you put the pictures in the same order?**

 

# Earthquake!

**In pairs, read the story. Then choose the correct form of the verbs, past simple or past continuous.**

**1** James ***did*** (M) / ***was doing*** (C) his homework in his bedroom when the earthquake ***started*** (H) / ***was starting*** (A) at 6.15 p.m.

**2** He ***sat*** (J) / ***was sitting*** (A) at his desk when the chair ***started*** (R) / ***was starting*** (A) to move across the floor.

**3** When the floor ***stopped*** (L) / ***was stopping*** (M) moving, James ***ran*** (E) / ***was running*** (R) to find his mother.

**4** His mother ***cooked*** (D) / ***was cooking*** (S) when the earthquake ***started*** (R) / ***was starting*** (S).

**5** When he ***found*** (I) / ***was finding*** (T) his mother, she ***stood*** (Y) / ***was standing*** (C) in front of the cooker.

She was OK, but the kitchen was a mess!

**6** They ***decided*** (H) / ***were deciding*** (R) to look outside. Outside, they ***saw*** (T) / ***were seeing*** (I) some trees on the ground and they heard voices calling for help.

**7** The hospital was very busy that evening, but nobody ***died*** (E) / ***was dying*** (N).

**8** It wasn't a very bad earthquake. It only ***measured*** (R) / ***was measuring*** (G) 5.5.

**Write the letters from over the correct answers to find out the name of the American scientist who invented a scale for measuring earthquakes in 1935.**

**C H** _ _ _ _ _ _ _ _ _ _ _ _ _ _ _

# Find Someone Who...

**1** **Find people who have done these things. Ask your classmates until you find one name for each thing.**

> **Example:** Have you eaten snails?
> **Yes, I have. / No, I haven't.**

**2** **In groups of four, find who has collected the most names.**

## Find someone who has...

**1** eaten snails ____________________
**2** received a letter today ____________________
**3** had a birthday in this month ____________________
**4** been to the USA ____________________
**5** baked a cake ____________________
**6** painted a wall ____________________
**7** drunk Chinese tea ____________________
**8** sung karaoke ____________________
**9** had an operation ____________________
**10** caught a bus to school today ____________________

**TIMESAVER GRAMMAR ACTIVITIES** Present perfect (questions)

# Find Someone Who...

**1** **Find people who have done these things. Ask your classmates until you find one name for each thing.**

> **Example:** Have you eaten snails?
> **Yes, I have. / No, I haven't.**

**2** **In groups of four, find who has collected the most names.**

## Find someone who has...

**1** eaten snails ____________________
**2** received a letter today ____________________
**3** had a birthday in this month ____________________
**4** been to the USA ____________________
**5** baked a cake ____________________
**6** painted a wall ____________________
**7** drunk Chinese tea ____________________
**8** sung karaoke ____________________
**9** had an operation ____________________
**10** caught a bus to school today ____________________

 

# Flags

**Colour the past participles in the boxes and find the flag. Then answer the question.**

## 1 What are the past participles of the verbs in the boxes?

Colour the past participles that end in ***-en*** → red

Leave all the other past participles → white.

**Which country's flag is this?**

--------------------------------------

| | | | | |
|---|---|---|---|---|
| begin | buy | come | do | drink |
| go | make | run | stand | throw |
| break | choose | drive | eat | fall |
| give | see | speak | steal | take |

## 2 What are the past participles of the verbs in the boxes?

Colour the past participles that end in:

***-ght*** → green

***-ed*** → white

***-t*** → orange

**Which country's flag is this?**

--------------------------------------

| | | | | | |
|---|---|---|---|---|---|
| catch | teach | walk | stop | lose | build |
| fight | buy | want | talk | feel | leave |
| bring | think | need | drop | send | sleep |

## 3 What are the past participles of the verbs in the boxes?

Colour the past participles that end in: *-ed* → red.

Colour the past participles that don't change their spelling → blue.

Leave all the other past participles → white.

**Which country's flag is this?**

--------------------------------------

| | | |
|---|---|---|
| hit | fall | watch |
| cost | get | play |
| cut | lose | change |
| put | send | cook |

# Around Australia

**1** **Begin at the START and read the sentences about Australia. Choose the correct question tag for each sentence. You will get to the FINISH if you go to all of the sentences once and choose the correct question tags.**

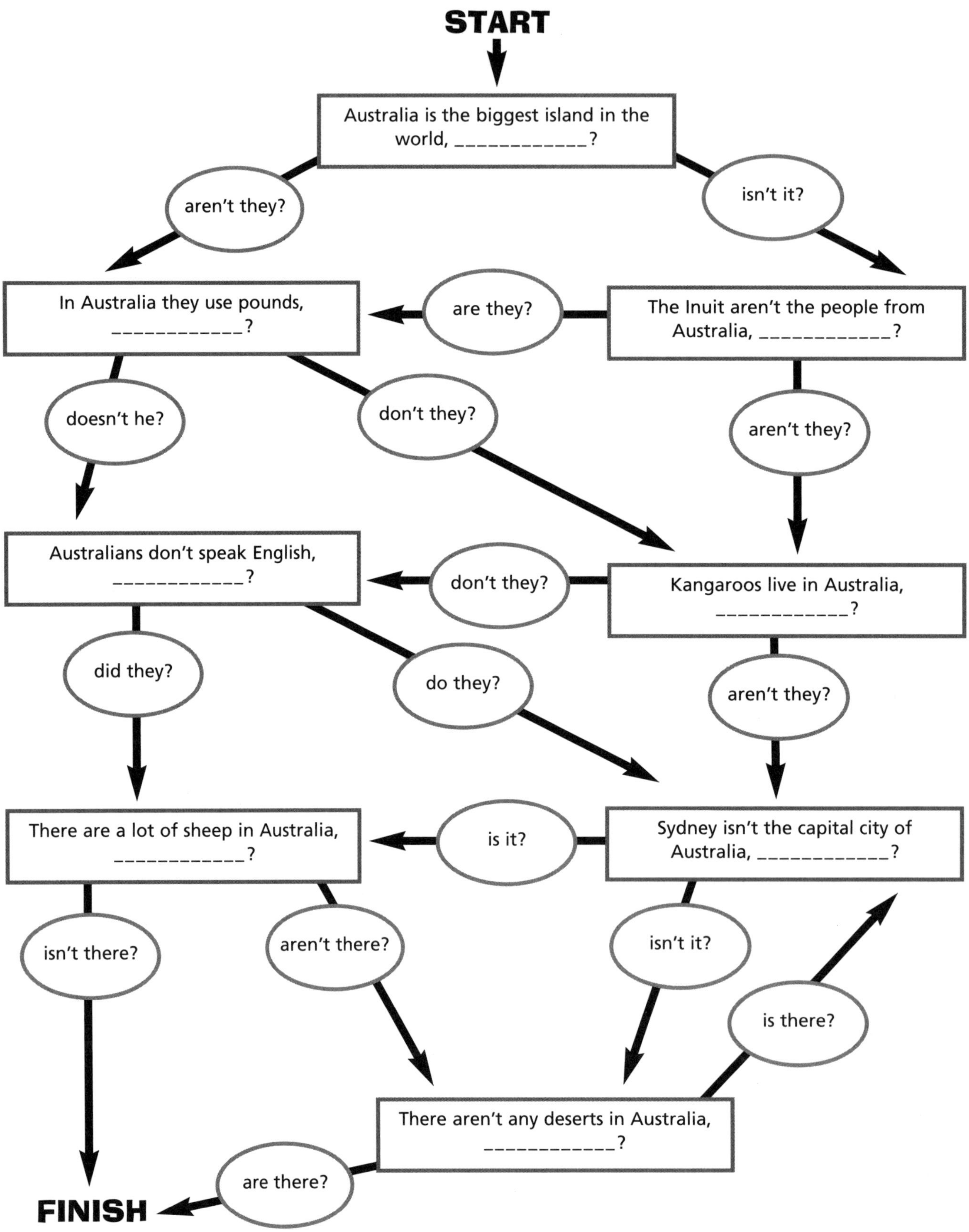


 

# Around Australia

**2** **Now write the questions with the correct question tags above the correct answers.**

1 Kangaroos live in Australia, don't they?

Yes, they do. You can only see them in Australia.

2 ______________________________

Yes, there are. There are 162 million sheep in Australia.

3 ______________________________

No, it isn't. Canberra is the capital city of Australia.

4 ______________________________

Yes, they do. They speak Australian English.

5 ______________________________

Yes, there are. There are 8 deserts.

6 ______________________________

No, they don't. They use the Australian dollar.

7 ______________________________

Yes, it is. But fewer people live in Australia than in the UK!

8 ______________________________

No, they aren't. The Aborigines are the indigenous people of Australia.

**3** **Compare your answers with your partner.**

# The Skiing Lesson

**Some teenagers are on a school skiing trip.**

**1** **Read the skiing instructor's sentences and choose the correct word for each sentence. Then circle the letter next to each correct word.**

**Example:** First, I want you to **put on** your skis.
(take off **V** / put on (**C**))

**1** Then, __________ me very carefully.
(listen to **H** / hear **A**)

**2** Can you all __________ me clearly?
(listen **E** / hear **A**)

**3** How many of you have __________ skiing before?
(gone **L** / been **M**)

**4** Have you ever __________ waterskiing or ice- skating before? Well, skiing is very similar.
(be **D** / been **O**)

**5** Now, we're at the top of a small hill. OK, let's try skiing down this hill towards that building over there. Can you __________ it?
(see **N** / look **I**)

**6** We all __________ mistakes, so don't worry if you fall over. (make **I** / do **S**)

**7** If you fall over, don't worry – I'll __________ you up! (take **R** / pick **X**)

**2** **What is the name of the ski resort?**
**Write the letters from inside the circles above to find the name of the ski resort.**
**The ski resort is**

(C) ( ) ( ) ( ) ( ) ( ) ( ) ( )

 

# Don't Make A Mistake!

**Read the clues and complete the crossword.**
**If you need help, the answers are at the bottom of this page.**
**Unscramble the letters to find the answer.**

## ACROSS

**1** Banks make a lot of ____________ .

**4** Study hard every day and you'll make good ____________ .

**5** That boy's got big ears, but don't make ____________ of him.

**6** Do you need help? Let me make a ____________ .

**7** Put a line through the word if you make a ____________ .

## DOWN

**1** Before you go on holiday, make a ____________ .

**2** Please tidy the room if you make a____________ .

**3** When you make a ____________ , you should keep it.

**5** Don't make a ____________ , I'll sort out the problem.

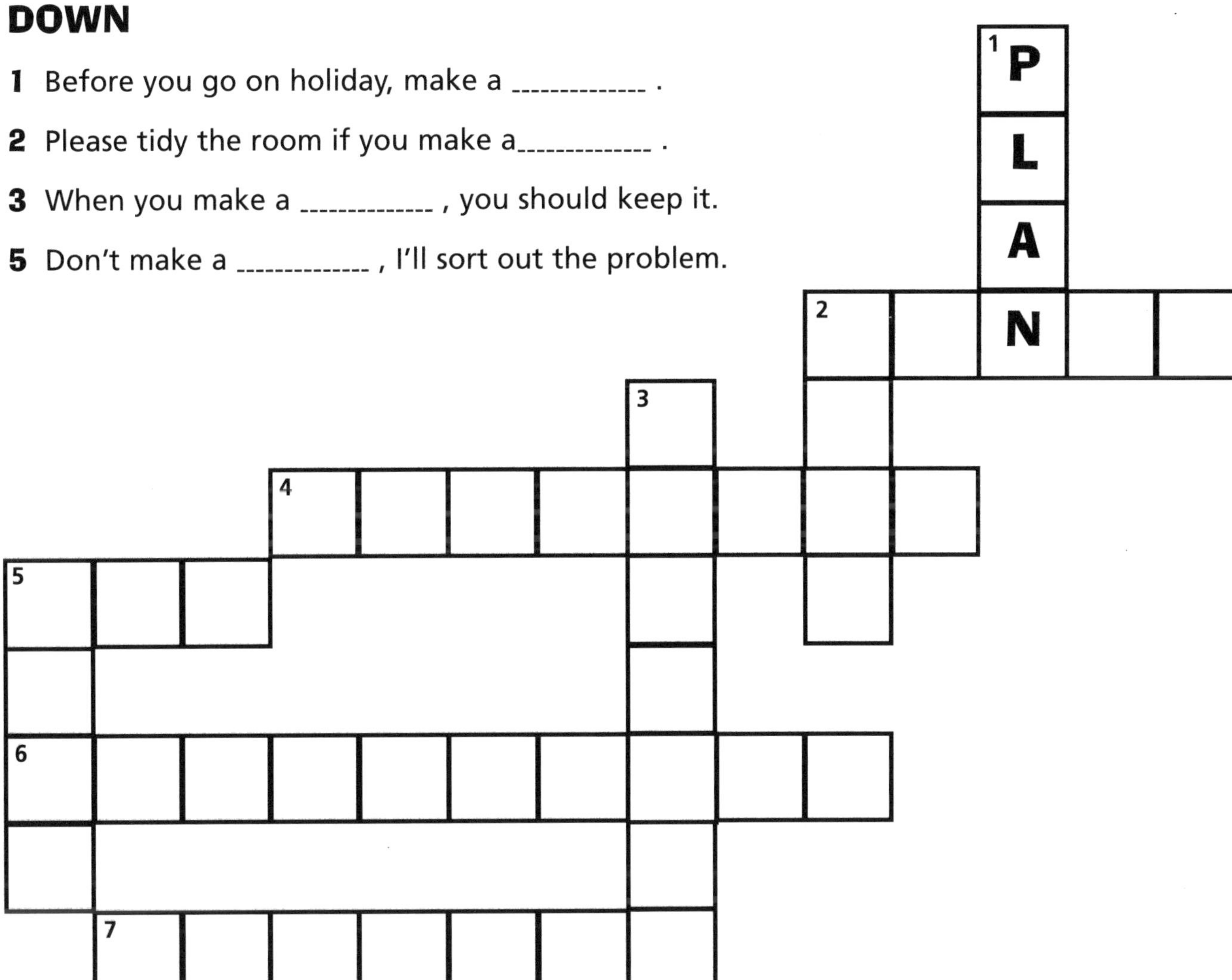


**ACROSS** **2** yemno **4** grospers **5** nfu **6** guessoting **7** staekim
**DOWN** **1** napl **2** sems **3** perosmi **5** sufs

# Do Me a Favour…

**Eric's mum wants Eric to help her on Saturday. She is thinking about what he can do.**

## 1 What is Eric's mum thinking? Match the sentences with the pictures.

1 He can do the washing-up. **C**
2 He can do the ironing. ____
3 He can do the shopping. ____
4 He can do the washing. ____
5 He can do the gardening. ____

A B C D E

## 2 It's Saturday, and Eric is talking to his mum. Complete the sentences with the expressions in the box.

| | |
|---|---|
| do the housework | ~~do me a favour~~ |
| do my homework | do my best |

**Mum:** Eric, will you *do me a favour* ?

**Eric:** I can't – I've got a maths test on Monday so I need to (1) ____ today, Mum.

**Mum:** Today? Saturday?

**Eric:** Yes, I've got a test! You always say that I've got to (2) ____ !

**Mum:** Yes, but…

**Eric:** But what, Mum?

**Mum:** You're right. I'll (3) ____

**Eric:** Thanks, Mum!

## 3 Who does the housework in your family?

**Write the names of the people in your family in the table. Tick (✓) the jobs that they do. Then compare your answers with a partner.**

| NAMES | | | | |
|---|---|---|---|---|
| cleaning | | | | |
| washing-up | | | | |
| washing clothes | | | | |
| ironing | | | | |
| gardening | | | | |
| shopping | | | | |

 

# Rules

**There are things that we must and mustn't do when we are in a park.**

**1** Read the signs in the park. Then match the signs with the people.

**2** Write what the people must or mustn't do. Use the words in the box.

**skateboard on the path** **wear shoes in the restaurant**
**pick flowers** ~~drop litter~~ **ride a bicycle on the path**
**walk on the grass** **let his dog play in the lake**
**wear a shirt in the restaurant**

Example: **TOM mustn't drop litter**

**TOM mustn't drop litter**

---

---

---

---

---

# English Class Rules

**What rules have you got in your English class? Write true sentences about your class.**

**1** **Complete our English Class Rules with *must* or *mustn't*.**

## Our English Class Rules

1 We ______ always speak in English.
2 We ______ laugh when the other students make mistakes.
3 We ______ eat sweets during the lesson.
4 We ______ look up new words in the dictionary.
5 We ______ always listen in our English class.
6 We ______ arrive late to class.
7 We ______ help each other in class.
8 We ______ do our homework.
9 We ______ help our English teacher.
10 We ______ shout.

**2** **Write three more rules for your English class. Compare your sentences with your partner.**

------------------------------------------------------------

------------------------------------------------------------

------------------------------------------------------------

 

# Does Mike Have to Cook Dinner?

## STUDENT A

Mike, Jeff, Paula and Tina are going camping.
Each person has to do two jobs.

### 1 Ask Student B questions to find out who has to do what. Tick (✔) the correct boxes.

Student A: Does Mike have to put up the tent?
Student B: No, he doesn't.
Student A: Does Mike have to build a fire?
Student B: Yes, he does.

| | Mike | Jeff | Paula | Tina |
|---|---|---|---|---|
| put up the tent | | | ✔ | ✔ |
| find wood | ✔ | | | |
| build a fire | | | | |
| get water | | ✔ | | |
| cook dinner | | | | |

### 2 Complete the sentences.

**Example:** Paula and Tina **have to put up** the tent, but **Mike** and **Jeff** don't have to.

**1** Mike and Jeff ____________ a fire, but Paula and Tina ____________

**2** Mike ____________ wood, but Jeff doesn't have to.

**3** Paula ____________ water, but Tina ____________

**4** Tina ____________ dinner, but her friends ____________

### 3 Who has to do these things?

**1** 'I have to put up the tent *and* get the water!'
____________

**2** 'Well, I have to put up the tent *and* cook dinner!'
____________

**3** 'I have to find wood *and* build a fire!'
____________

**4** 'Well, I have to build a fire, too!'
____________

## STUDENT B

Mike, Jeff, Paula and Tina are going camping.
Each person has to do two jobs.

### 1 Ask Student A questions to find out who has to do what. Tick (✔) the correct boxes.

Student B: Does Jeff have to cook dinner?
Student B: No, he doesn't.
Student A: Does Paula have to put up the tent?
Student B: Yes, she does.

| | Mike | Jeff | Paula | Tina |
|---|---|---|---|---|
| put up the tent | | | | |
| find wood | | | | |
| build a fire | ✔ | ✔ | | |
| get water | | | ✔ | |
| cook dinner | | | | ✔ |

### 2 Complete the sentences.

**Example:** Paula and Tina **have to put up** the tent, but **Mike** and **Jeff** don't have to.

**1** Mike and Jeff ____________ a fire, but Paula and Tina ____________

**2** Mike ____________ wood, but Jeff doesn't have to.

**3** Paula ____________ water, but Tina ____________

**4** Tina ____________ dinner, but her friends ____________

### 3 Who has to do these things?

**1** 'I have to put up the tent *and* get the water!'
____________

**2** 'Well, I have to put up the tent *and* cook dinner!'
____________

**3** 'I have to find wood *and* build a fire!'
____________

**4** 'Well, I have to build a fire, too!'
____________

# Lost At Sea

**Vincent and Casper are on a desert island and their ship is lost. Vincent is hungry, wet and dirty. He lost his two front teeth in the storm and all they've got to eat is an apple and a pot of yoghurt. They are having a conversation. He says to Casper *I want …*, and Casper always answers *But you need …***

**1** Complete the crossword. The clues are what Vincent wants to do. Casper's answers are the things he needs.

**ACROSS**

1 brush my teeth 

3 wash my dirty hands 

4 dry my face 

6 change my clothes and go to bed 

10 be dry when it rains tonight 

13 drink some tea 

14 go home 

16 cook some supper 

**DOWN**

1 bite into this apple 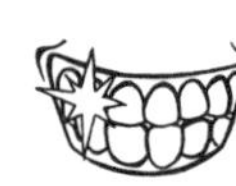

2 wash my hair 

3 have a wash 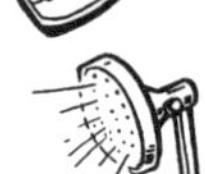

5 know what the time is 

7 dry my hair 

8 cut this apple into pieces 

9 walk across the island 

11 make some toast 

12 eat this yoghurt 

**2** In pairs, practise saying Vincent and Casper's conversation.

**Example:** **(Vincent) I want to bite into this apple.**
**(Casper) You need teeth!**

# What Should I Do?

1. In groups of five, cut out the *Problem* and the *Suggestion* cards.
2. Mix up the *Suggestion* cards and give them to the rest of the group.
3. In turns, students read a *Problem* card to the group. The group listens and reads the correct *Suggestion* cards.
The group can invent its own suggestions when there are no more cards.

**PROBLEM 1**

**Please help! My dog, Sniff, doesn't like my best friend. Every time my friend comes to my house, Sniff jumps up and barks loudly. Sniff's a good dog, but when my friend comes, he isn't very nice. My friend is afraid. What should I do?**

**PROBLEM 2**

**Help me! My mother is very strange. She's got really bad breath because she eats onions for breakfast every day. And she's the singing teacher at my school! Everybody laughs and jokes about 'Mrs Onion'. Mum says that onions are good for you. Now she wants me to start eating onions, too! What should I do?**

**PROBLEM 3**

**Please help! I've got a problem. I live in a flat and my aunt and uncle live in the flat upstairs. In my bedroom, I can hear them talking. Last night, my uncle said to my aunt, 'The police don't know. Nobody knows – only you and me!' I'm worried. What should I do?**

 

# Suggestion Cards

| | | |
|---|---|---|
| leave the dog outside | stay at a friend's house for a week | ask your aunt about it |
| tell your friend how to behave with your dog | throw the onions away | talk to your uncle |
| teach the dog to be good | soak the onions in water every night – then they won't be as strong | tell your parents |
| leave the dog in a room and close the door | eat the onions and enjoy them! | watch your uncle very carefully |
| give your dog its food when your friend arrives | buy a lot of chewing gum | call the police |
| get a new dog | tell everybody at school that onions are good for you | move to a different bedroom |

# World of Animals Maze

**Begin at the START sentence and follow the maze. If you think the sentence is true, follow the black arrow. If you think the sentence is false, follow the white arrow. You will get to the FINISH if you go to all of the sentences once and make the right decisions. Good luck!**

9 Owls can hear very soft sounds that people can't hear.
11 A grass snake's bite can kill people.
Finish
2 Cats can see very well at night.
5 Dogs can hear some high sounds that people can't hear.
6 Giraffes can make a loud, trumpeting noise
3 Snakes can close their eyes.

# Snap!

**Play this game in groups of three. You need: 1 dice and 1 counter for each player. One person, who doesn't play, is the referee. The referee has the Answer Key.**

**STUDENT A**

**REFEREE'S ANSWER KEY**

1. THE GIRL IS LOOKING AT THE STARS.
2. THE BOY IS LOOKING AT A MAP.
3. THE GIRL IS LOOKING AT A PAINTING.
4. THE BOY WATCHING TV.
5. THE GIRL IS WATCHING A BALLET.
6. THE BOY AND GIRL ARE WATCHING A FOOTBALL MATCH.
7. THE BOY IS LISTENING TO A CD.
8. THE GIRL IS LISTENING TO HER GRANDFATHER.
9. THE BOY AND GIRL ARE LISTENING TO THE RADIO.
10. THE BOY CAN HEAR A TELEPHONE.
11. THE GIRL CAN HEAR AN AMBULANCE.
12. THE BOY AND GIRL CAN HEAR A DOG.

 

**How to play Snap!**

- Cut out the picture cards for Student A and the verb cards for Student B.
- The players turn over their cards one card at a time and put them face-up in two separate piles on the table.
- When the picture and the verb cards go together, the first player to say 'Snap!' has to say what the person in the picture is doing.
- Student C, the referee, says if the answer is correct or not.
- If the answer is correct, the player keeps the two cards.
- If the answer is wrong, the cards go back to the bottom of the picture and verb piles.

When the players haven't got any more cards, they pick up their piles, mix their cards up, and continue playing.

- The winner is the player who wins all of the cards. Then the winner plays against Student C and the loser becomes the referee.
- REMEMBER: We use all of the verbs in the continuous form except hear: ~~He is hearing as~~ → He can hear a …

**STUDENT B**

| | | | |
|---|---|---|---|
| LOOKING AT | LOOKING AT | LOOKING AT | WATCHING |
| WATCHING | WATCHING | LISTENING TO | LISTENING TO |
| LISTENING TO | CAN HEAR | CAN HEAR | CAN HEAR |

# Birthdays

**Today is 3rd December. Read the conversation and write the names on the calendar.**

| | |
|---|---|
| **Katie:** | Happy birthday, Susan! |
| **Susan:** | Thanks, Katie. When's your birthday? |
| **Katie:** | It's tomorrow. |
| **Susan:** | Oh, great! Did you know that David's birthday is the day after tomorrow? |
| **Katie:** | Is it? Tim and Leo's birthdays are at the weekend. Leo's is on the day after Tim's. |
| **Susan:** | What a lot of birthdays in December! Sandra's birthday is a week tomorrow and John's is two weeks on Friday. |
| **Katie:** | Wow! And Fiona's is on Christmas Day! |
| **Susan:** | James' birthday is next month. It's the day after New Year's Day. |
| **Katie:** | Oh, and I just remembered – Richard's birthday is next Monday. |
| **Susan:** | That's right! And Laura's is two weeks today. |
| **Katie:** | People born in December are the best, don't you think? |
| **Susan:** | Definitely! |

## CALENDAR

### DECEMBER

| Sun | Mon | Tues | Weds | Thurs | Fri | Sat |
|---|---|---|---|---|---|---|
| 1 | 2 | 3 *Susan* | 4 *Katie* | 5 | 6 | 7 |
| 8 | 9 | 10 | 11 | 12 | 13 | 14 |
| 15 | 16 | 17 | 18 | 19 | 20 | 21 |
| 22 | 23 | 24 | 25 | 26 | 27 | 28 |
| 29 | 30 | 31 | | | | |

### JANUARY

| Sun | Mon | Tues | Weds | Thurs | Fri | Sat |
|---|---|---|---|---|---|---|
| | | | 1 | 2 | 3 | 4 |
| 5 | 6 | 7 | 8 | 9 | 10 | 11 |
| 12 | 13 | 14 | 15 | 16 | 17 | 18 |
| 19 | 20 | 21 | 22 | 23 | 24 | 25 |
| 26 | 27 | 28 | 29 | 30 | 31 | |

 

# What Do You Do...?

**1 Read the questions and circle the best word: *when* or *while*.**

**1** What do you do ***when*** **/ *while*** the phone rings?
**a.** run and answer it immediately
**b.** wait and listen to the person on the answering machine
**c.** wait for somebody else to answer the phone

**2** What do you do ***when / while*** you're waiting at the dentist's?
**a.** read a magazine
**b.** bite your fingernails
**c.** think about your last visit to the dentist

**3** What do you do ***when / while*** you're sitting on an aeroplane for four hours?
**a.** read a good long book
**b.** play games
**c.** sleep

**4** What do you do ***when / while*** you can't find your trainers?
**a.** look for them until you find them
**b.** ask your Mum where they are
**c.** get angry

**5** What do you do ***when / while*** you are studying for a very difficult exam?
**a.** close the door and work quietly
**b.** listen to the radio and study at the same time
**c.** stop every ten minutes to get a drink

**6** What do you do ***when / while*** your bicycle doesn't work?
**a.** get some tools and mend the bicycle
**b.** wait for your dad to mend the bicycle
**c.** get angry

**2 For each question choose the answer which best describes what you would do. Then read the personality analysis below.**

**Add up your score and find out about your personality.**

**A = 2 points B = 1 point C = 0 points**

**10–12 points**
You're very sensible. You like to do things well.

**7–9 points**
Sometimes you're a bit lazy.

**4–6 points**
You want life to be easy. You don't want to work hard for things.

**1–3 points**
You're lazy! You need to be a bit more energetic!

# Truth and Lies

**Have they told the truth?**

**1** Look at the pictures on the left. Write the question in each speech bubble.

**2** Write the answer for each picture.
Choose the correct answers from the box.

**1** you / clean / your room / yet?

**2** the postman / come / yet?

**3** your mum / give / you any pocket money yet?

**4** do / the washing up / yet?

**5** your sister / make / the breakfast / yet?

**6** you / finish / on the phone / yet?

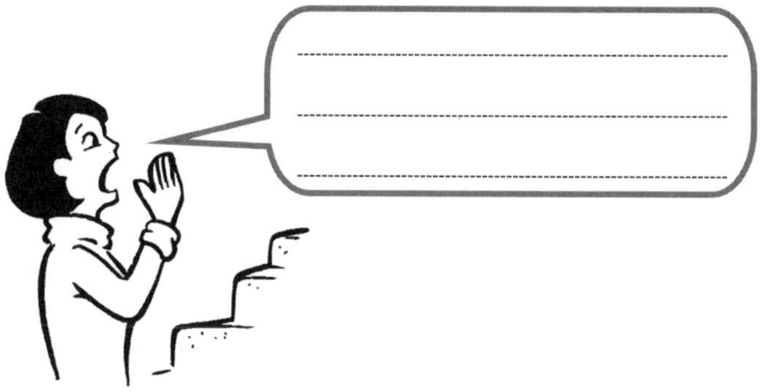

 

# ANSWER

Yes, we've already eaten it.
No, not yet. Can I have some?
Yes, I've already said goodbye.
~~Yes, I've already done it~~.
Yes, and I've already put everything away.
No, he hasn't come yet.

1

**Yes, I've already done it.**

2

3

4

5

6

## 3 Four of the answers are lies. Write the true answers.

**1** No, I haven't done it yet.

**2**

**3**

**4**

# Facts and Figures

**How many questions can you answer correctly?**

**1** **Can you count the objects in CAPITAL letters?**
**No □ write *much*. Yes □ write *many*.**

1 How __many__ EGGS are there in 1 dozen?
2 How __much__ SUGAR can you put in a 1 kg bag?
3 How _______ HOURS are there in a day?
4 How _______ MINUTES are there in half an hour?
5 How _______ MONTHS are there in a year?
6 How _______ WATER can you put in a 2 litre bottle?
7 How _______ DAYS are there in 1 week?
8 How _______ TIME do you have for your lunchbreak at school?
9 How _______ CHILDREN are there in your class?
10 How _______ CENTIMETRES are there in 1 metre?
11 How _______ CENTS are there in $1?
12 How _______ MONEY is £1 in your country?
13 How _______ PENCE are there in £10?
14 How _______ BUTTER is there in two 500g packets?
15 How _______ ORANGE JUICE is there in six 1 litre cartons?

**2** **Now write the answers to the questions. Then compare your answers with your partner. Your teacher will tell you the answers. Who's got the most correct answers, you or your partner?**

1 12 eggs ______________________________
2 1 kg ______________________________
3 ______________________________
4 ______________________________
5 ______________________________
6 ______________________________
7 ______________________________
8 ______________________________
9 ______________________________
10 ______________________________
11 ______________________________
12 ______________________________
13 ______________________________
14 ______________________________
15 ______________________________

 

# Who is the Most Polite?

**1** Write what the people are saying. Use the words in the grid to write the sentences.

| | A | B | C | D | E |
|---|---|---|---|---|---|
| 1 | OPEN | CAN | YES | CAN'T | BORROW |
| 2 | YOU | ASK | PLEASE | ME | CAMERA |
| 3 | I | GIVE | YOUR | THE | POLITELY |
| 4 | WINDOW | ? | . | , | NO |

**1**

B1 – A3 – E1 – C3 – E2 – B4

C1 – D4 – A2 – B1 – C4

Lydia

Megan

Lydia: Can I borrow your camera?

Megan: 

**2**

B1 – A3 – A1 – D3 – A4 – D4 – C2 – B4

E4 – D4 – A2 – D1 – C4

Tim

Miss Jones

Tim:

Miss Jones:

**3**

B3 – D2 – C3 – E2 – C4

E4 – D4 – B2 – D2 – E3 – C4

Rich

Liam

Rich: 

Liam: 

**2** Read the conversations in exercise 1 again and answer the questions.

**1** Who is the most polite?

**2** Who isn't very polite?

**3** In pairs, invent polite requests for these situations.

**1** You're cold. You want to shut the door.
**2** You've lost your bus ticket. You want to borrow money from a friend to buy another ticket.
**3** You're feeling ill. You want to leave the classroom for a while.

# What Would You Like...?

**1** **Look at the pictures and circle the things that you like.**

chocolate

tomatoes
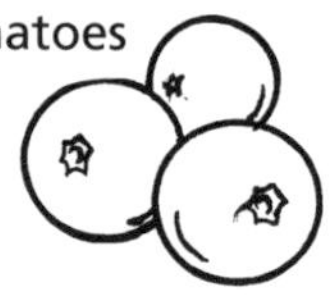
onions

cheese

crisps

sugar

**Would you like this food on a pizza?**

**2** **Do you like doing these things? Look at the pictures and circle the things that you like doing.**

sitting by the fire

eating ice-cream

drinking hot chocolate

having a picnic

eating hot food

**Would you like to do these things on a cold, snowy day?**

**3** **Look at the pictures and circle the animals that you like.**

snake

dog

horse

spider

rabbit
cat

**Which of these animals would you like to have as a pet?**

 

# Class Survey

**1** Do this class survey in small groups.
Complete the questions in the class questionnaire with *Who* or *Whose*.

**2** Check your answers with your group. Does everybody in your group agree?

| | | NAMES |
|---|---|---|
| 1 ______________ | home is the nearest to school? | |
| 2 ______________ | was born in summer? | |
| 3 ______________ | favourite colour is blue? | |
| 4 ______________ | goes to music lessons after school? | |
| 5 ______________ | can play the guitar? | |
| 6 ______________ | writes with their left hand? | |
| 7 ______________ | birthday is in winter? | |
| 8 ______________ | parents can speak English very well? | |

## Guess who...?

**3** In your group, decide which of your classmates' names to write as the answer for each question.

**4** Now ask the students whose names you wrote. Are your answers correct?

**Example:** Olga, is your home the nearest to school?
If the answer is 'No', ask another student. Find the correct name for every question.

## Feedback

**5** In your groups, compare your answers. How many names did you complete? How many answers were correct?

**6** Which group had the most correct answers? The group with the most correct answers is the winner.

## Make your own questionnaire

**7** Write four questions with *who* and four questions with *whose*.

**8** In pairs, read each other's questionnaires. Answer the questions with your classmates' names.

**9** Then ask the students whose names you wrote. Are your answers correct?

 

# Penpals

**1** Read Simon's letter to his new penpal, Karl.

*Dear Karl,*

*I'm 13 years old and I live in England. My English teacher gave me your address. I would like to be your penpal.*

*I never stay still. I go shopping every Saturday with my friends. I go swimming with my mum after school on Wednesdays. I go horse-riding on Sundays and I go ice-skating after school on Tuesdays. I go dancing on Saturday nights with my friends. I walk my dog, Curly, every evening after dinner.*

*What do you do? Please write back.*

*Your friend,*
*Simon*

**2** Tick the boxes for the days when Simon does these things.

| | **Monday** | **Tuesday** | **Wednesday** | **Thursday** | **Friday** | **Saturday** | **Sunday** |
|---|---|---|---|---|---|---|---|
| shopping | | | | | | ✔ | |
| swimming | | | | | | | |
| dancing | | | | | | | |
| ice-skating | | | | | | | |
| running | | | | | | | |
| horse-riding | | | | | | | |
| walk the dog | | | | | | | |

**3** Now write **ME** in the boxes for the days when you do these things.

**4** Compare your answers with other students in the class. Does anybody do exactly the same things as you?

**Example:** When do you go shopping?
I go shopping every Saturday.

**5** Write a letter to a penpal. Describe the things that you do every week.

 

# Do You Like...?

**1** **Complete the questionnaire. Tick *love, like, don't like* or *hate*.**

**2** **In pairs, ask questions to find five things that you both feel the same about. Then compare your questionnaires and check your answers.**

**Example:** Do you like clothes shopping?
No, I don't. / Yes, I do.

| | **love** | **like** | **don't like** | **hate** |
|---|---|---|---|---|
| clothes shopping | | | | |
| strawberry ice-cream | | | | |
| cooking | | | | |
| collecting stamps | | | | |
| football | | | | |
| Leonardo DiCaprio | | | | |
| Shania Twain | | | | |
| eating meat | | | | |
| reading books | | | | |
| computer games | | | | |
| police action films | | | | |
| wearing hats | | | | |

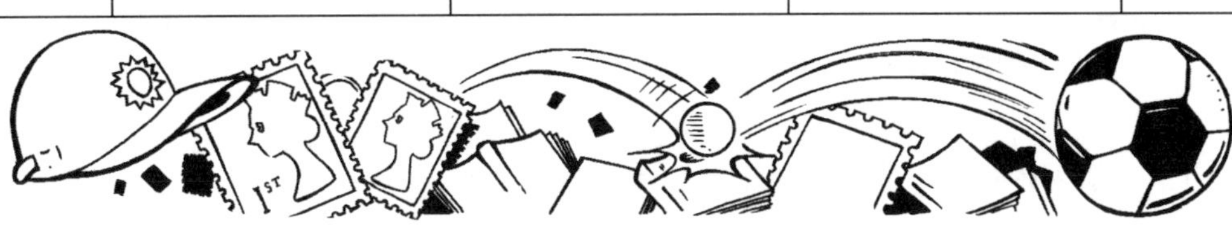

# Where Do People…?

**1** **Look at the pictures and write questions with *Where*.**

**1** eat / sushi
**Where do people eat sushi?**
--------------------------------------------

**2** speak / Welsh
--------------------------------------------
--------------------------------------------

**3** see / kangaroos
--------------------------------------------
--------------------------------------------

**4** play / the bagpipes
--------------------------------------------
--------------------------------------------

**5** visit / the Pyramids
--------------------------------------------
--------------------------------------------

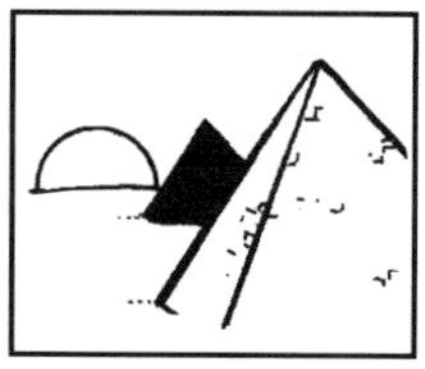

**6** celebrate / the 4th of July
--------------------------------------------
--------------------------------------------

**7** dance / the flamenco
--------------------------------------------
--------------------------------------------

**8** grow / tea
--------------------------------------------
--------------------------------------------

**2** **Now compare your answers with your partner.**

**3** **Take it in turns to ask and answer the questions. Can you answer all of the questions?**

**4** **Check your answers!**
**Complete the crossword with the names of the countries from exercise 1.**

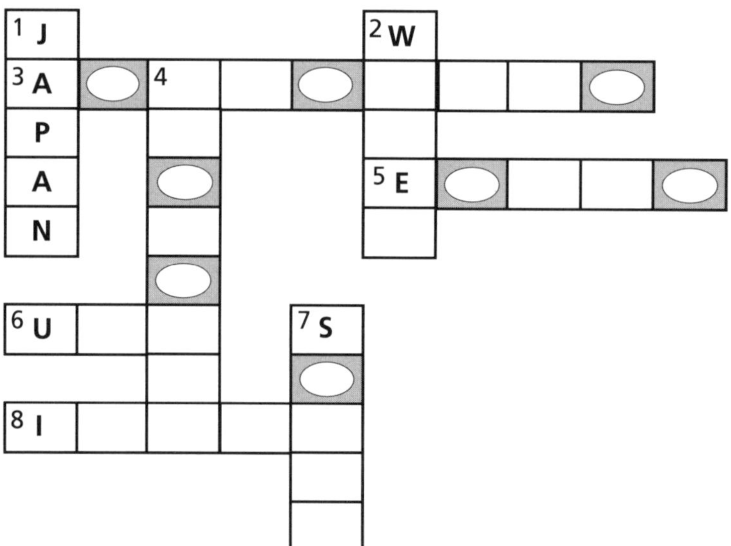


**5** **Where do people sing 'fado'?**
**Write the letters from inside the circles in the crossword. Unscramble the letters to find out where people sing 'fado'.**

People sing 'fado' in

# A Strange Letter

**Can you read this letter?**

**In pairs, read the letter. Use the key on the right of the page to understand the code. Then write your answers below each question in the letter.**

Write full sentences: ~~Yes, I am~~. → Yes, I am listening.

You are reading a secret letter.

U R  ə  

R U  ?

R U  ?

B ə   U ?

R U  + ə  ?

B UU    ?

 B UU   ?

**CODE KEY**

| | |
|---|---|
| a | ə |
| are | R |
| eating |  |
| English |  |
| from |  |
| god |  |
| is | B |
| learning |  |
| letter |  |
| partner |  |
| reading |  |
| secret |  |
| sitting down |  |
| sun |  |
| teacher |  |
| watching |  |
| wearing | 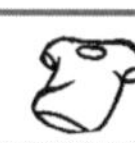 |
| what |  |
| with | + |
| working |  |
| you | U |
| your | UU |

# Shopping For The Family

**Mr Gonzalez is visiting London. He's got shopping lists from his wife, his son and his daughter.**

**1** Write *a* or *an* by the things in the lists.

| | | |
|---|---|---|
| 1 ...a... bottle of perfume<br>2 ...an... Agnës B skirt<br>3 ................ pink leather handbag<br>4 ................ silk scarf<br>5 ................ ink pen | 6 ............ electric shaver<br>7 ............ new PlayStation game<br>8 ............ Oasis CD<br>9 ............ Arsenal Football Club scarf<br>10 ............ comedy video | 11 ............ animal poster<br>12 ............ English magazine<br>13 ............ teddy bear<br>14 ............ easy jigsaw puzzle<br>15 ............ pair of trainers |

**2** Now find the pictures and write the numbers.

**3** Look at the five pictures that haven't got a number. These are the things that Mr Gonzalez wants to buy for himself. Write Mr Gonzalez's list.

1 **an umbrella**
2 ................
3 ................
4 ................
5 ................

# These Aren't My Things!

**Grandma tidied the house today, but Colin and his sister, Victoria, aren't happy. Grandma put some of Victoria's things in Colin's room.**

**1** **Look at the picture and write three sentences about Victoria's things in each speech bubble.**

**Example:** This isn't my skirt, it's hers!

1 ____________________________________

2 ____________________________________

3 ____________________________________

**Example:** These aren't my shoes, they're hers!

4 ____________________________________

5 ____________________________________

6 ____________________________________

**There are some strange things in Colin's bedroom.**

**2** **Complete the conversation between Colin and his mother with *that* and *those*.**

**Mother:** Colin, what's (1) __________ under your bed?

**Colin:** (2) __________'s my rat. He's my best friend.

**Mother:** And Colin, what are (3) __________?

**Colin:** Do you mean (4) __________ spiders?

**Mother:** Spiders?

**Colin:** Yes, they're my new pets. (5) __________ one's name is Creepy.

**Mother:** (6) __________ rat and (7) __________ spiders are going outside. Now!

  

# A Sleepover

**Amy is sleeping over at her friend Rebecca's house this weekend.**

**1** Look at the picture. Amy is packing her suitcase. What is she taking with her? Choose the correct words from the box and write them in the correct suitcase.

**toothbrush / money / CDs / magazines / sweets / keys
sports clothes / passport / mobile phone / make-up / homework / tennis racket / pyjamas / swimming costume / book**

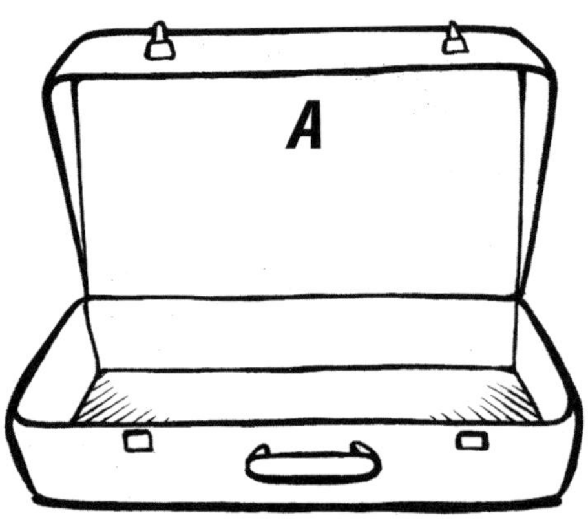

**2** What things isn't she taking? Write the words from the box in the sentences.

**She isn't taking any ______________, ______________, ______________, or ______________. She isn't taking a ______________ or a ______________.**

 

**3** Rebecca's mum is making breakfast. Read her question and Amy's answer. Then look at the pictures. Which is Amy's breakfast?

**4** Write your own answer to the question and draw your breakfast on the empty plate.

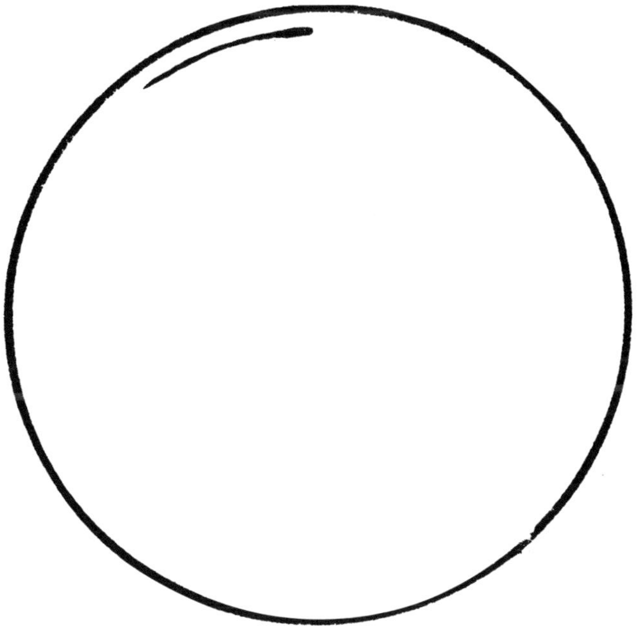

# Charlotte's or Charles'?

**Each person has got something that belongs to another person. Who has got Charles' football? Who has got Charlotte's shoes? Look at the picture and write a sentence about each person.**

**Example:** Charles **has got Charlotte's ballet shoes.**

1. Tess has got ______________________________
2. Victoria ______________________________
3. James ______________________________
4. Charlotte ______________________________
5. Peter ______________________________

 

# Christmas presents

**What did Marie's family get for Christmas?**

**1** **Match the people in Marie's family with their Christmas presents.**

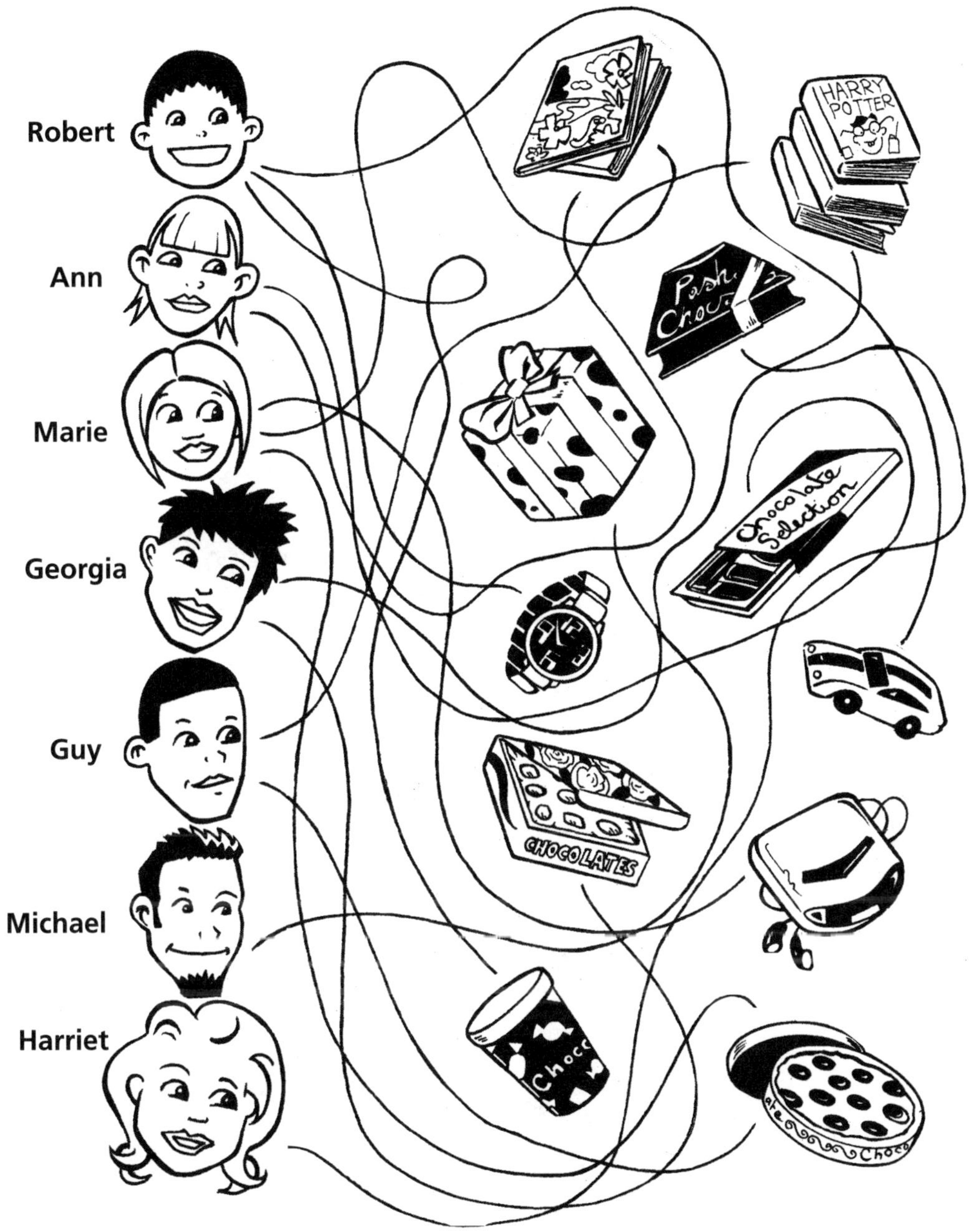


**2** **Complete the sentences about what Marie's family got for Christmas. Use *mine, yours, his, hers, ours* and *theirs*.**

**Example:** This is Robert's watch. And this car is *his* too.

1 My sister Ann and I love reading! The books are ________.

2 Georgia and Guy have got books too, but ________ are in English.

3 We all got chocolates for Christmas. Harriet's eating ________ now!

4 And look at this CD player – it's ________!

5 And what about you, Michael? What's ________?

# Word Chain

**1** **Complete the name of the things in the pictures.**
**Use the words in the box to form compound nouns.**

| | | |
|---|---|---|
| bag | board | kart |
| ball | bulb | phones |
| ~~bath~~ | book | post |
| bell | case | ring |
| bin | cup | stop |

**1 bubble** bath

**2 door** ..........

**3 ear** ..........

**4 go-** ..........

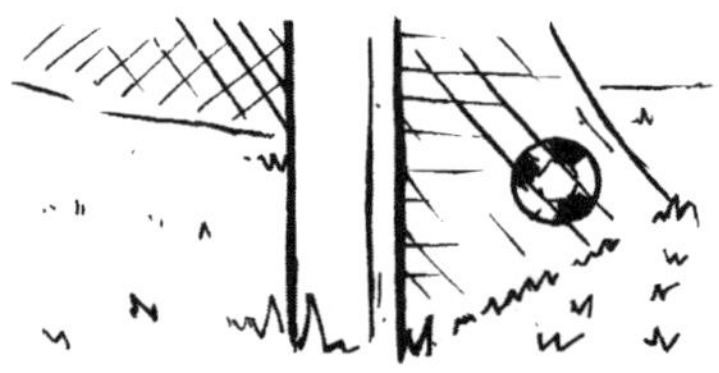

**5 goal** ..........

**6 head** ..........

**7 key** ..........

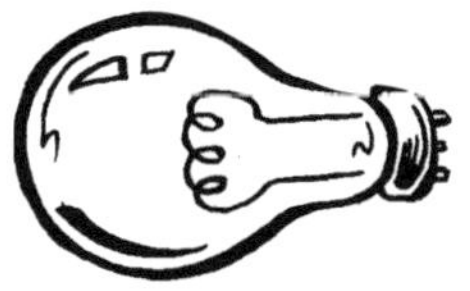

**8 light** ..........

**9 litter** ..........

**10 tea** ..........

**11 note** ..........

**12 pencil** ..........

**13 school** ..........

**14 tennis** ..........

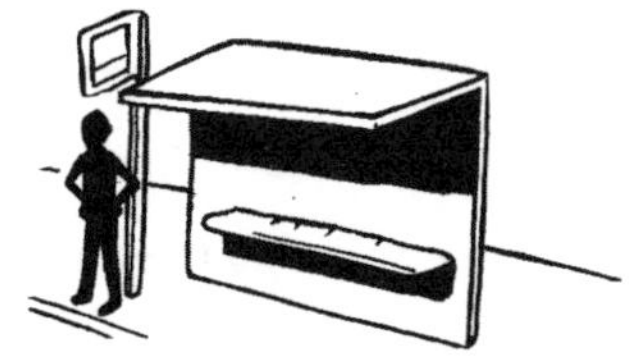

**15 bus** ..........

 

**2** **Write the words in the word chain.**
**The last letter of a word is the first letter of the next word.**

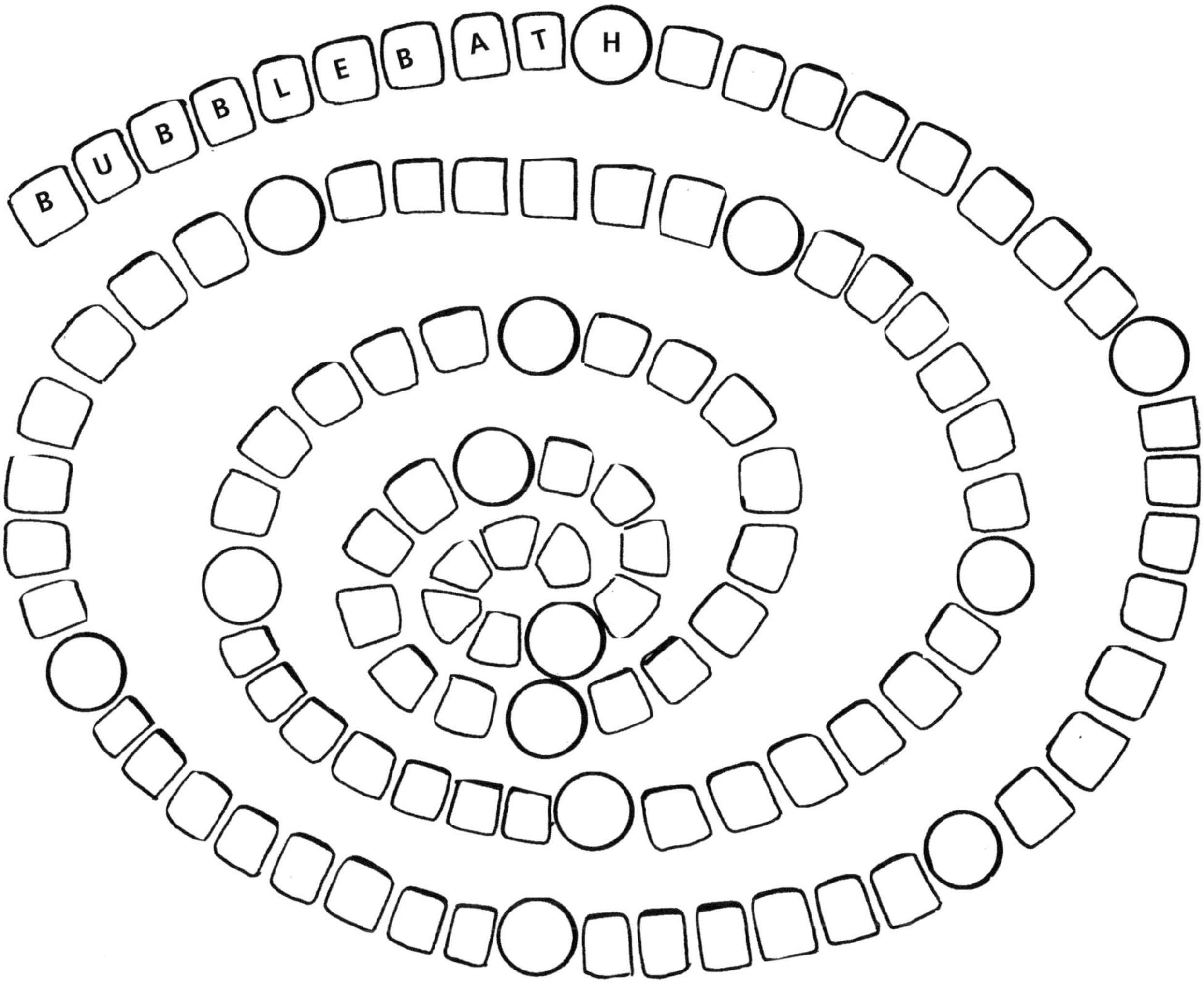


**3** **How many more compound nouns can you make?**
**Use the words in the box and continue the list.**

**teabag, football, bathroom**

# Double or Nothing

**Play this game in small groups. You need: 1 die and 1 counter for each player. One person, who doesn't play, is the referee. The referee has the Answer key.**

**How to play Double or Nothing**

Roll the die and move your counter. When you land on a picture, say: 'I see two ...' and spell the word. The referee tells you if you are correct or not.

**Scoring**
Correct answer = 2 points.
Wrong answer = 0 points.
The player with the most points wins.

**Example: I see two babies: b - a - b - i- e - s. (correct)**

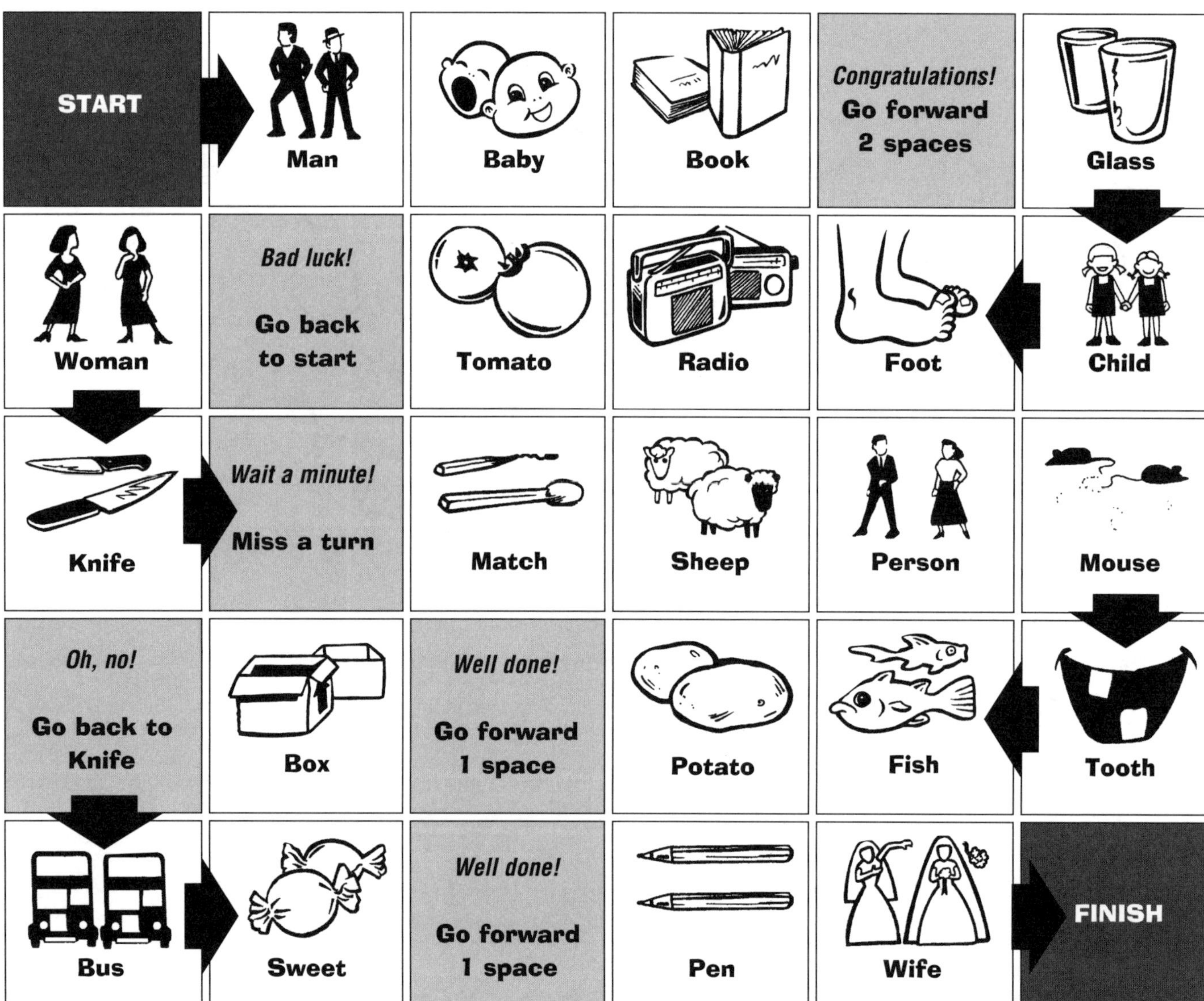


**REFEREE'S ANSWER KEY** man – men baby – babies book – books glass – glasses child – children foot – feet radio – radios tomato – tomatoes woman – women knife – knives match – matches sheep – sheep person – people mouse – mice tooth – teeth fish – fish potato – potatoes box – boxes bus – buses sweet – sweets pen – pens wife – wives

 

# Around The World

**1** Find the names of twenty countries in the wordsearch. ⇨ ⇩

**2** What languages do these students speak?

| | | | | | | | | | | | |
|---|---|---|---|---|---|---|---|---|---|---|---|
| I | R | E | L | A | N | D | O | T | S | U | E |
| T | L | E | M | B | G | E | R | M | A | N | Y |
| A | U | S | T | R | A | L | I | A | P | I | E |
| L | S | H | G | P | U | N | M | K | A | T | R |
| Y | F | C | E | O | B | E | W | A | L | E | S |
| S | C | O | T | L | A | N | D | S | T | D | Y |
| B | C | S | P | A | I | N | N | P | O | S | C |
| E | W | R | O | N | T | S | F | R | A | T | A |
| L | I | T | R | D | K | O | R | E | A | A | N |
| G | J | A | T | H | M | S | A | R | U | T | A |
| I | A | M | U | K | O | R | N | T | N | E | D |
| U | P | E | G | R | E | E | C | E | O | S | A |
| M | A | N | A | T | A | Y | E | G | R | O | I |
| E | N | G | L | A | N | D | D | E | W | F | A |
| C | E | I | S | R | I | K | E | O | A | M | P |
| H | T | H | A | I | L | A | N | D | Y | E | T |
| I | R | U | S | S | I | A | M | Y | E | N | O |

1 German ____________

3 ____________

4 ____________

2 ____________

5 ____________

# California or Florida?

**How much do you know about these two American states? Look at the map.**

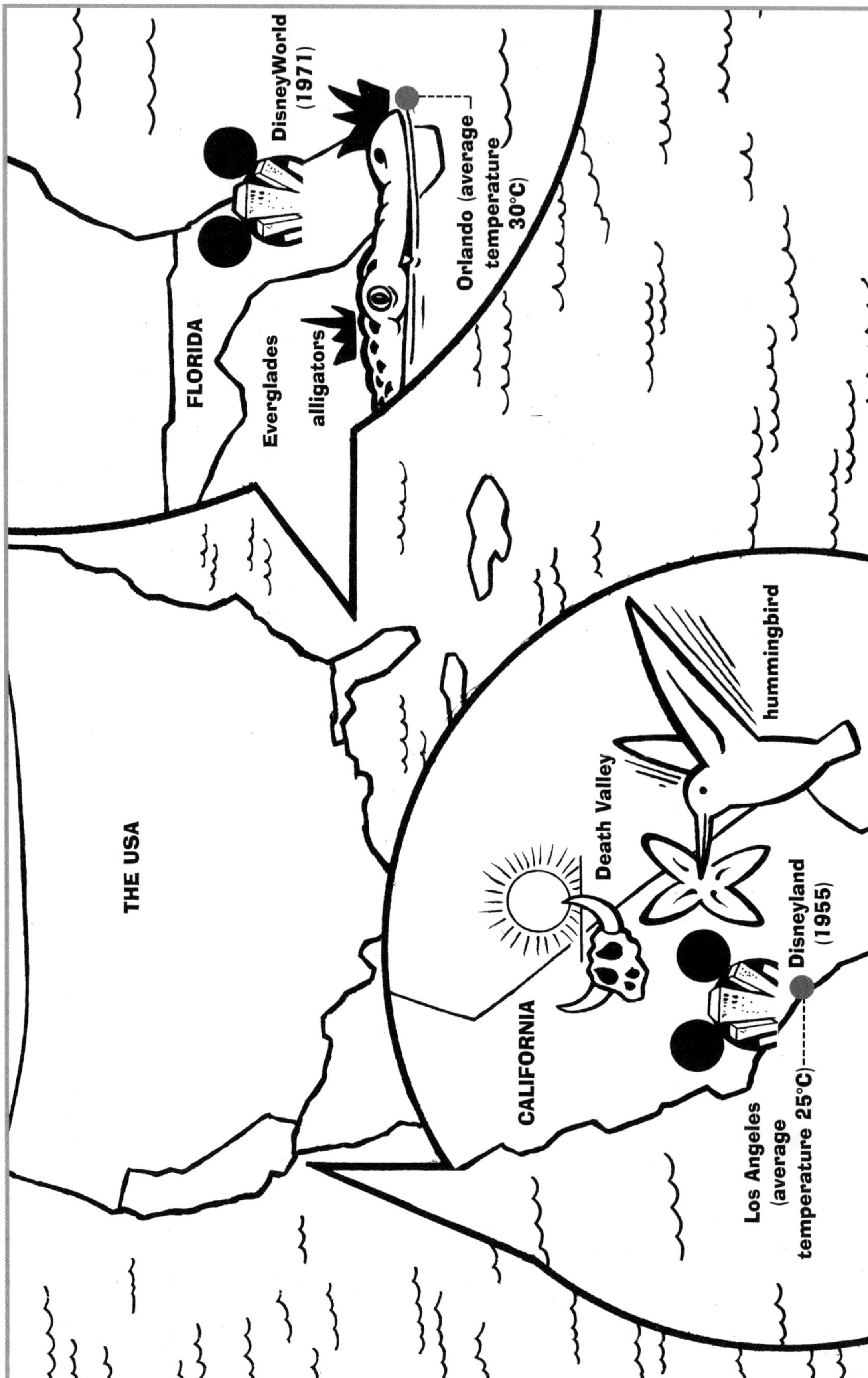


 

Cut out the cards and turn them over. In pairs, take it in turns to turn over two cards and read them aloud. If they are both correct or both wrong, the player keeps the cards and takes another turn. The player with the most pairs of cards is the winner.

| | | |
|---|---|---|
| Florida is smaller than California. | Disneyland, California is older than DisneyWorld, Florida. | An alligator is longer than a hummingbird. |
| Death Valley is wetter than the Everglades. | Orlando is hotter than Los Angeles. | California is bigger than Florida. |
| Orlando is colder than Los Angeles. | Death Valley is drier than the Everglades. | Florida is bigger than California. |
| An alligator is smaller than a hummingbird. | Los Angeles is warmer than Orlando. | DisneyWorld, Florida is older than Disneyland, California. |

# Good and Bad Habits

**Play this game in small groups. You need: 1 die and 1 counter for each player.**

### How to play Good and Bad Habits

**1** Each player rolls the die and moves following the arrows on the board.

**2** When you stop on a Habit square, read out the habit aloud. All of the players decide if it is a good habit or a bad habit. If it is a good habit, move forward 2 squares. If it is a bad habit, move back 3 squares.

**3** The first player to arrive at the Prize-giving Ceremony wins!

| | | | |
|---|---|---|---|
| START | | You always brush your teeth after you eat a meal. | |
| | You often forget your pens and school books. | | |
| You often leave the milk out of the fridge. | | | |
| You never eat fresh fruit and vegetables. | | You sometimes write on your desk. | |
| | You usually play your CDs very loudly. | You never clean your shoes. | |

| | | | |
|---|---|---|---|
| | You never push other students in the lunch queue. | | You usually wash your face before you go to bed. |
| | | You are always polite to your teachers. | |
|  | | | You sometimes help your parents on Saturdays. |
| | | You always wash your hands before you eat. | |
| You never tell lies. | | You always do your homework. | You usually put away your clothes and tidy your room. |

# What Are They Doing?

**Write sentences about what the people are doing. Use the verbs in the box and change the correct adjective from each pair into the adverb form.**

crying ~~helping~~ laughing playing playing running sharing shouting

**1**

**polite – rude**

He's helping an old lady politely.

**2**

**generous – mean**

**3**

**beautiful – terrible**

**4**

**slow – quick**

**5**

**angry – calm**

**6**

**sad – happy**

**7**

**quiet – loud**

**8**

**bad – good**

 

# Who Lives the Most Dangerously?

**1 Work in small groups. Read the questions and complete the table with *1–5*. Write *1* for the least up to *5* for the most. Everyone in your group must agree.**

- Which sports person can jump the highest?
- Which sports person can run the fastest?
- Which sports person lives the most dangerously?
- Which sports person takes the most exercise?
- Which sports person has to think the most carefully?

| | can jump the highest | can run the fastest | lives the most dangerously | takes the most exercise | has to think the most carefully |
|---|---|---|---|---|---|
| a footballer | | | | | |
| a dancer | | | | | |
| a swimmer | | | | | |
| a mountain climber | | | | | |
| a golfer | | | | | |

**2 Now compare your answers with another group.**

**3 Write the names of the other people in your group and complete the table with *1–5*. Write *1* for the least up to *5* for the most. Then compare your table with the others in your group. Do you all agree?**

**I think that Simon is the most generous. What do you think?**

| | does the best homework | is the most generous | can jump the highest | can run the fastest | takes the most exercise |
|---|---|---|---|---|---|
| | | | | | |
| | | | | | |
| | | | | | |
| | | | | | |
| | | | | | |

# Put Away the Shopping!

## STUDENT A

**1** **Student B has bought some food. Look at the fridge and tell Student B where to put the food in the fridge. Use the words in the boxes.**

**Example:** Put the carrots on the bottom shelf, on the right.

| | | |
|---|---|---|
| *on the left* | *in the middle* | *on the right* |

| | | | | |
|---|---|---|---|---|
| ~~carrots~~ | butter | tomatoes | chicken | lettuce |
| eggs | yoghurt | cheese | sausages | |

# Put Away the Shopping!

## STUDENT B

**1** **You have bought the food in the box. Listen to Student A. Write the food words in the correct place in the fridge.**

**Example:** Put the carrots on the bottom shelf, on the right.

| | | | | |
|---|---|---|---|---|
| carrots | butter | tomatoes | chicken | lettuce |
| eggs | yoghurt | cheese | sausages | |

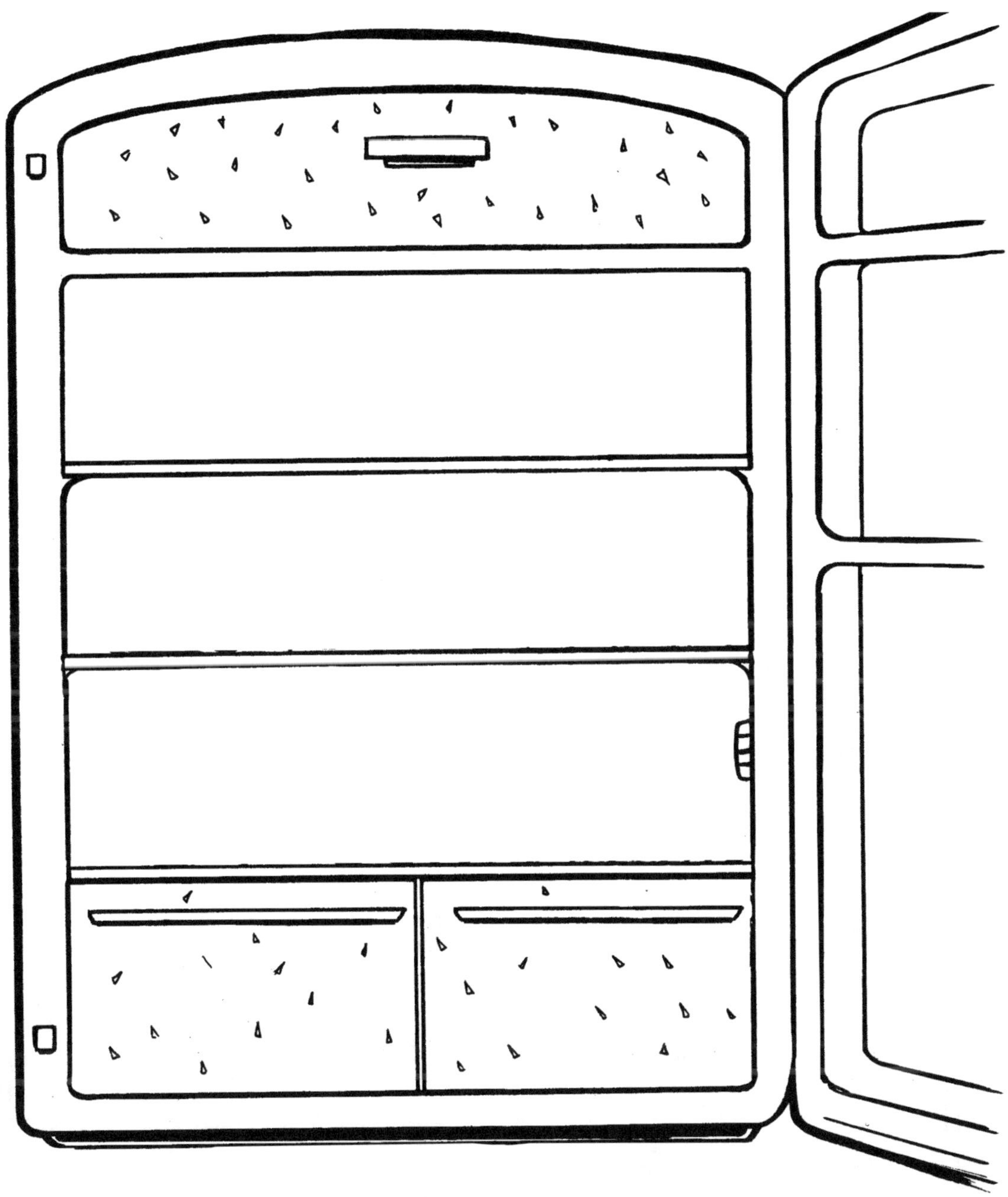

**2** **Compare your fridge with Student A's fridge. Have you put the shopping in the correct places?**

# A Class Trip

**You and your classmates are going to a museum by coach.**

**1** You are sitting in seat 7. Write your name on your seat. Imagine who is sitting near you on the coach and write your classmates' names on their seats.

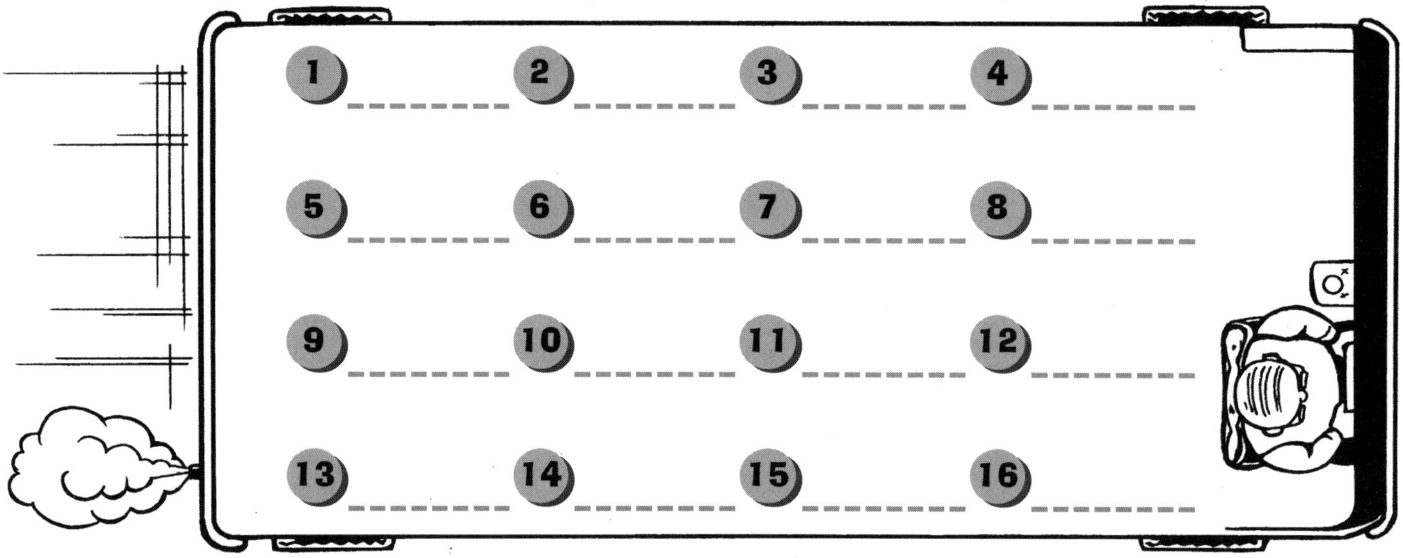


**1** Who is sitting next to you? ____________

**2** Who is sitting behind you? ____________

**3** Who is sitting in front of you? ____________

**2** Ask a classmate about their coach. Listen carefully. Write the names on the correct seats. Is your coach the same as theirs? Use *next to / behind / in front of*.

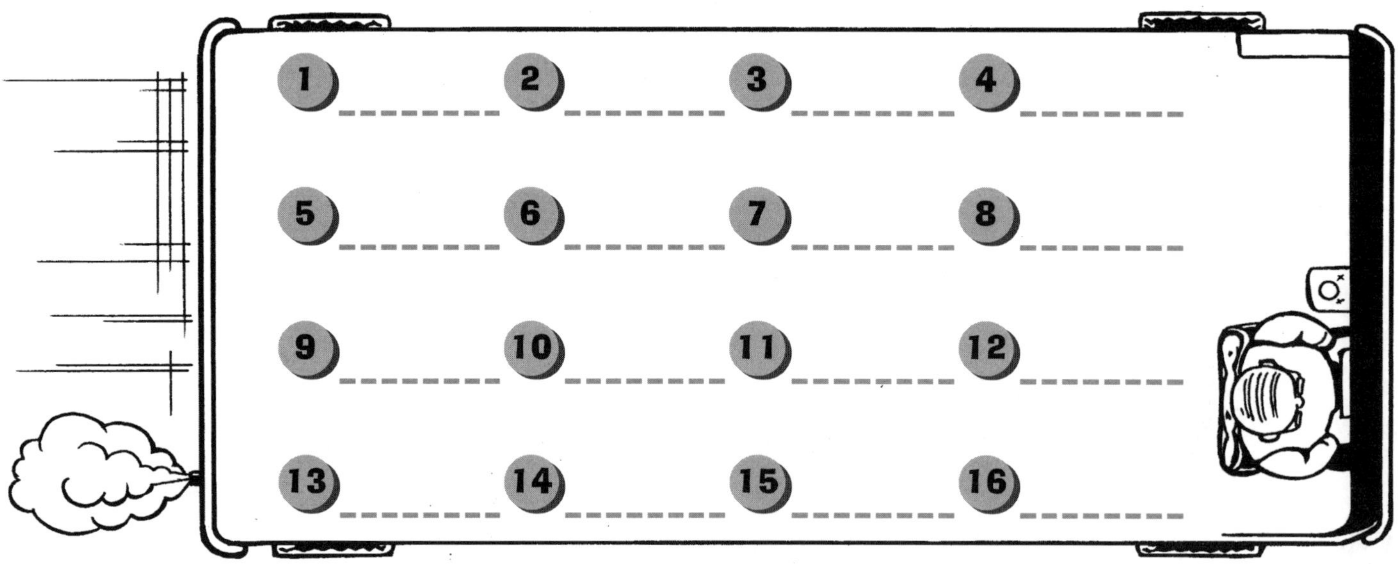


 

# Put Your Clothes Away!

**1** Match the pictures with the sentences.

**1** She's folding up the sweatshirt.
**2** She's putting away the hat.
**3** She's zipping up her jacket.
**4** She's putting on the sweatshirt.
**5** She's trying on the hat.
**6** She's taking off the sweatshirt.

**2** Look at the boys getting ready for swimming. Write the correct name under each boy in the picture.

**Tony is taking his glasses off.**

**Jason can't swim very well, so he's putting his armbands on.**

**Graham is folding his trousers up and Callum is folding his shirt up.**

**Dean is trying Callum's swimming goggles on.**

**The swimming coach is zipping his tracksuit up and is shouting, 'Hurry up, Ricky! Put your homework away or I'll take it away!'**

**Ricky is putting away his homework so the coach doesn't take it.**

**3** Underline the two parts of every multi-word verb in the sentences above.

# Give in your Homework, Please

**Read the sentences. Complete the crossword with the missing verbs from the multi-word verbs.**

**Across**

4. If you're very noisy, the teacher will __________ you off.
5. __________ away all of your rubbish now.
7. __________ out your mistakes with a rubber.
9. Don't put your coat on the floor. __________ it up.
10. __________ off your personal stereo and listen to me.

**Down**

1. When you finish, __________ in your exercise books.
2. Don't write. __________ your pens down.
3. It's dark in here. Please __________ on the light.
6. You can __________ out the answer by adding and dividing.
8. __________ away your calculators. You don't need them today.

# Help!

**Allie the alien is visiting Earth for the first time.
There are a lot of things that she doesn't know how to do!**

**1** Complete Allie's sentences with the multi-word verbs from the box.

**turn over    turn down    turn off    turn on**

**1 I don't know how to ____________ the water!**

**2 I don't know how to ____________ the TV!**

**3 I don't know how to ____________ this cassette! I want to play the other side.**

**4 I don't know how to ____________ the music!**

**2** Look at the pictures of James and his baby brother, Sam. What can't Sam do? Write a sentence about Sam under each picture. Use *He can't* with the phrasal verbs in the box.

**do up    tidy up    pick up    put on**

1

2

3

4

# The Beach Towel Mystery

1. Put the words on the towels in the correct order.
2. Follow the footprints in the sand to put the story in the correct order.
3. Now write the complete story in the correct order.

**S** stole Who things? her

______________________
______________________
______________________

**A** left towel. earrings her and her Michelle her watch on

______________________
______________________
______________________

**E** swimming the all went in sea. They

______________________
______________________
______________________

**G** something she came When was back, wrong.

______________________
______________________
______________________

 

**L** beach. But there was the else on nobody

______________________

______________________

______________________

**L** too. earrings her And missing, were

______________________

______________________

______________________

**START**

**S** went friends Eight beach. to the

______________________

______________________

______________________

**U** watch. couldn't She her find

______________________

______________________

______________________

**3** **Look at the letters next to each towel. Write the letters in the correct order to solve the mystery word.**

**The S _ _ _ _ _ _ _ stole Michelle's things!**

# Friends

**Help Julia to write her diary. Put the word in the correct space to complete each sentence. You've got a time limit of three minutes. The first student to complete all of the sentences is the winner!**

**1** I __usually__ watch TV in the evening ________ . *(usually)*
**2** My ________ TV show ________ is *Friends*. *(favourite)*
**3** My mother ________ watches *Friends* ________ . *(never)*
**4** She doesn't understand why ________ I ________ like to watch it. *(always)*
**5** But perhaps it isn't for ________ women ________ ! *(old)*
**6** My mother isn't ________ old ________, but she isn't young. *(very)*
**7** Perhaps she's ________ intelligent ________ than me! *(more)*
**8** And perhaps I'll listen to her and not ________ watch ________ much TV. *(so)*
**9** But ________ , I've got to watch ________ *Friends*. *(first)*

**10** Oh, no! Mum ________ is watching it ________! (now)

# Classrooms

**1** There are ten differences between Classroom A and Classroom B. Read the example and find nine more differences. Write sentences with *but*.

**Example: In Classroom A there are frogs in the aquarium, but in Classroom B there are fish in the aquarium.**

**2** Compare your answers with your partner. Did you find the same things?

# A Seaside Holiday

**Spot the difference – Student A**

**1** **Look at your picture. Student B has got a similar picture. Can you find eleven differences?**

**Example:** **STUDENT A** In picture A, there are **three** boys on the beach.
**STUDENT B** In picture B, there are **two** boys on the beach.

**2** **Now compare your picture with Student B's.**

 

# A Seaside Holiday

**Spot the difference – Student B**

**1** **Look at your picture. Student A has got a similar picture. Can you find eleven differences?**

> **Example:** **STUDENT A** In picture A, there are **three** boys on the beach.
> **STUDENT B** In picture B, there are **two** boys on the beach.

**2** **Now compare your picture with Student A's.**

# What was there...?

**STUDENT A**

**What was there after the robbery?**

**Look at the picture of what there was before the robbery. Ask Student B questions to find out what there was after the robbery. There are ten differences between your picture and Student B's picture. Read the example and find nine more differences.**

**Example:** **Student A:** There were some paintings on the walls yesterday.
**Student B:** There aren't any paintings now.

**YESTERDAY**

# What was there...?

**STUDENT B**

**What was there before the robbery?**

**Look at the picture of what there was after the robbery. Ask Student A questions to find out what there was before the robbery. There are ten differences between your picture and Student A's picture. Read the example and find nine more differences.**

**Example: Student A:** There were some paintings on the walls yesterday.
**Student B:** There aren't any paintings now.

**NOW**

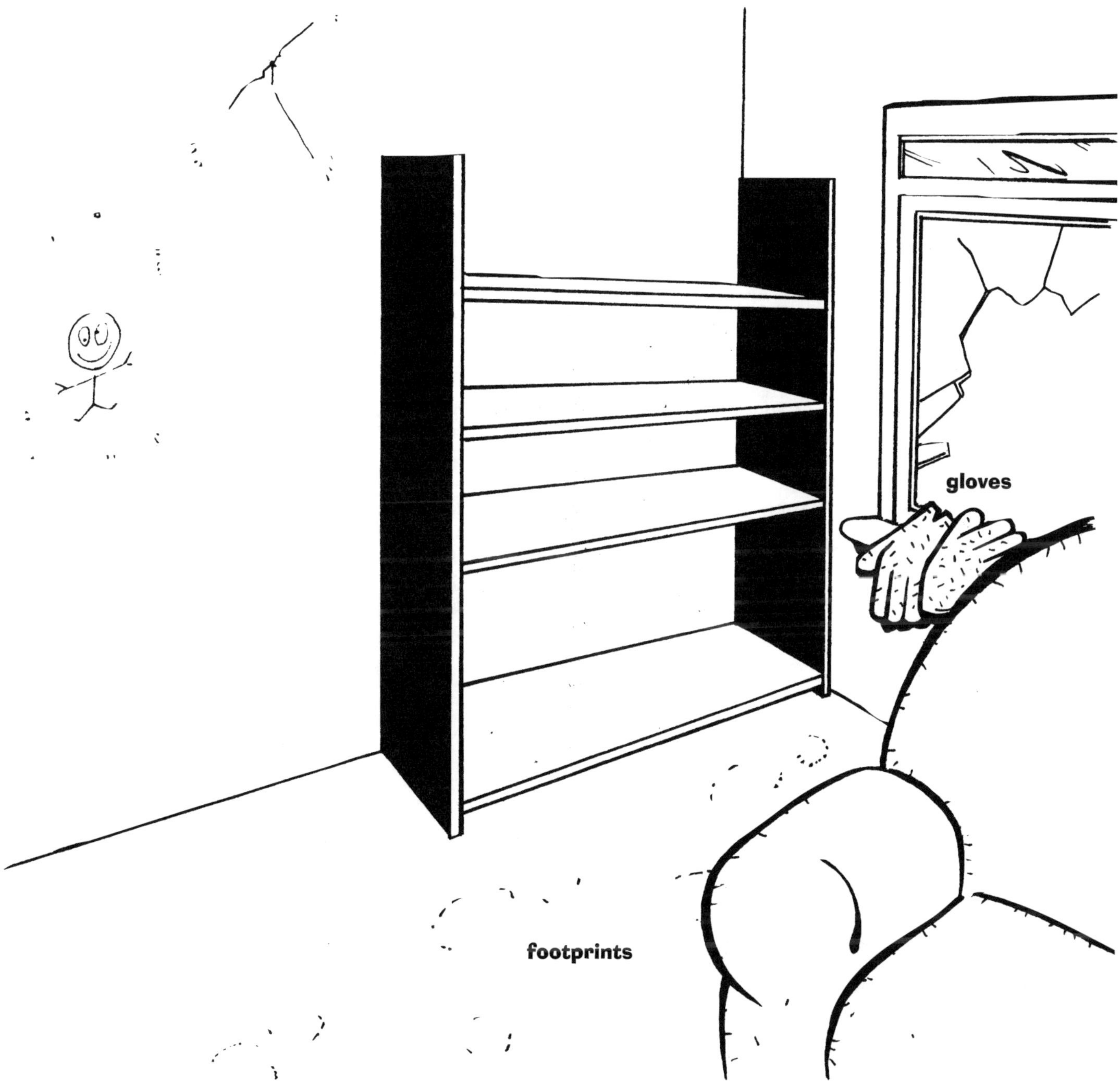

**PAGES 4 & 5 Have You Got The Basketball?**

Students' own answers.

**PAGES 6, 7 & 8 English Families**

Students' own answers.

**PAGE 9 Wild Animals in North America**

| | | | | |
|---|---|---|---|---|
| 1. come | 2. has | 3. can't | 4. stay | 5. lives |
| 6. has got | 7. uses | 8. doesn't go away | | 9. eat |
| 10. look | 11. are | 12. stay | 13. don't like | |
| 14. prefer | 15. are | 16. eat | 17. is | |
| A. 2 | B. 3 | C. 1 | | |

**PAGE 10 The Pet Game**

Students' own answers.

**PAGE 11 After School**

**1.** 1. play tennis
2. watches TV
3. rides his bicycle
4. plays the guitar
5. plays computer games
6. reads magazines
7. goes swimming
8. telephones

**2.** Students' own answers.

**PAGE 12 Getting To Know Someone**

**1.**

| | | | | |
|---|---|---|---|---|
| 1. Are | 2. do | 3. are | 4. Are | 5. Does |
| 6. Are | 7. Do | 8. Are | 9. Do | 10. Do |
| 11. Are | 12. Do | 13. Is | 14. Do | 15. Do |
| 16. Do | 17. Is | 18. Are | 19. Do | 20. do |

**2. & 3.** Students' own answers.

**PAGE 13 In Britain**

2. Yes, we have.
3. Yes, you are.
4. Yes, I am.
5. No, you don't.
6. No, we haven't.

**PAGE 14 Get Fit!**

1. He usually eats chips. Today, he's eating a banana.
2. He usually plays computer games. Today, he's playing tennis.
3. He usually eats pizza. Today, he's eating salad.
4. He usually plays cards. Today, he's playing basketball.
5. He usually reads comics. Today, he's exercising.
6. He usually watches TV. Today, he's swimming.

**PAGE 15 Our World**

The answers are on the Referee's Answer Key.

**PAGE 16 Bananas in Pyjamas**

| | | | |
|---|---|---|---|
| A. sprinkle | B. brush | C. dip | D. roll up |
| 1. B | 2. I | 3. G | 4. D |
| 5. H | 6. L | 7. J | 8. E |
| 9. C | 10. F | 11. K | 12. A |

**PAGE 17 When I Grow Up**

**1.** A. rabbits B. coins C. magic D. cards E. never

**2.** magician

**3.** 2. He's going to be a pilot.
3. He's going to be a teacher.
4. She's going to be a comedian.
5. She's going to be an artist.
6. She's going to be a musician.

**PAGE 18 The Crystal Ball**

Students' own answers.

**PAGE 19 The Future is in your Hands**

Students' own answers.

**PAGE 20 What time...?**

**1.**

| | | |
|---|---|---|
| 1. check in | 2. takes off | 3. arrive |
| 4. does … leave | 5. departs | 6. leave |
| 7. goes | 8. stops | 9. change |
| 10. does … get | 11. takes | 12. collects |
| 13. arrive | 14. does … start | 15. do … open |

**2.** B. Ian C. Gary D. Mum E. Alice F. Laura G. John

**PAGE 21 The Marie Celeste**

**1.**

| | | | | |
|---|---|---|---|---|
| 1. was | 2. was | 3. was | 4. were | 5. were |
| 6. was | 7. was | 8. were | 9. was | 10. was |
| 11. was | 12. was | 13. were | 14. were | 15. was |
| 16. Was | 17. was | | | |

**2.** There are three wrong things in the picture:
1. The fire isn't out.
2. The year is the diary is 1875 – it should be 1872.
3. The date is the diary is 23 November – it should be 25 November.

 

## PAGE 22 Cookery Crossword

**1. + 2.** 2. mixed 3. added 4. sprinkled
5. cooked 6. turned 7. lifted 8. enjoyed

**3.** OMELETTE

## PAGE 23 Story Puzzle

**1.**

**2.** The correct order for the story is:

8. My little sister cried because she wanted to play in the park.
10. 'Why are you crying again?' I asked her.
3. Mum dried my sister's eyes with a tissue. 'OK, let's go to the park,' said Mum.
1. The taxi stopped next to us.
6. My little sister and I jumped into the taxi.
4. 'Mum, you dropped some money. It's under the driver's seat!' I said.
7. Mum used her umbrella to get the money.
5. Mum paid the driver £6.80. Then we ran into the park.
2. I played in the park with my sister for an hour.
9. Then I carried my sister home because Mum hadn't got any more money for a taxi!

## PAGE 24 Yesterday at the Fair

**1.**

A. She bought two balloons.
B. She drank a can of Cola.
C. She ate a candy floss.
D. She went on the big wheel twice.
E. She had one go at throwing the ring and she won a teddy bear.
F. She went on the rollercoaster three times.

**2.** Jessica spent £21.95 at the fair.

## PAGE 25 The Hare and the Tortoise

1. could 2. was 3. said 4. had
5. found 6. told 7. hid 8. began
9. ran 10. was 11. thought
12. fell 13. woke up 14. saw 15. wasn't
16. was 17. ran 18. couldn't
19. sat 20. had 21. got up 22. came
23. won

## PAGE 26 The Fishing Trip

**1.** 2. caught; helped
3. tried; turned
4. swam; held
5. took
6. said; left; could

**2.** 1. C 2. D 3. E 4. B 5. A 6. F

## PAGE 27 Earthquake!

1. was doing; started
2. was sitting; started
3. stopped; ran
4. was cooking; started
5. found; was standing
6. decided; saw
7. died
8. measured

The inventor of the Richter scale is CHARLES RICHTER.

## PAGE 28 Find Someone Who ...

Students' own answers.

## PAGE 29 Flags

1. Poland
2. Ireland
3. France

## PAGES 30 & 31 Around Australia

2. There are a lot of sheep in Australia, aren't there?
3. Sydney isn't the capital city of Australia, is it?
4. Australians don't speak English, do they?
5. There aren't any deserts in Australia, are there?
6. In Australia they use the pound, don't they?
7. Australia is the biggest island in the world, isn't it?
8. The Inuit aren't the indigenous people of Australia, are they?

## PAGE 32 The Skiing Lesson

**1.** 1. listen to 2. hear 3. been 4. been 5. see 6. make 7.pick

**2.** CHAMONIX

## PAGE 33 Don't Make a Mistake!

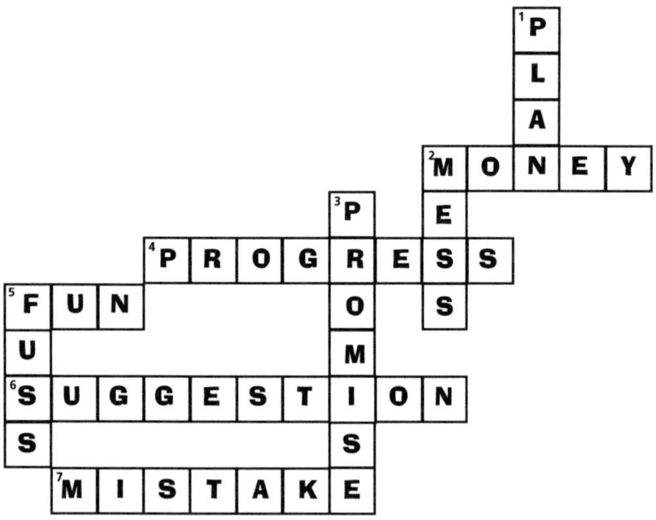

## PAGE 34 Do Me a Favour

**1.** 1. C 2. E 3. B 4. D 5. A

**2.**

1. do my homework
2. do my best
3. do the housework

**3.** Students' own answers.

## PAGE 35 Rules

**1.** 2. Robert; Tom 3. Lucy; Richard 4. Anna; Stephen 5. Liz 6. Dan

**2.** Stephen mustn't skateboard on the path.
Lucy must wear shoes in the restaurant.
Liz mustn't pick flowers.
Anna mustn't ride a bicycle on the path.
Robert and Tom mustn't walk on the grass.
Dan mustn't let his dog play in the lake.
Richard must wear a shirt in the restaurant.

## PAGE 36 English Class Rules

Students' own answers.

## PAGE 37 Does Mike have to cook dinner?

**1.**

| | Mike | Jeff | Paula | Tina |
|---|---|---|---|---|
| put up the tent | | | ✔ | ✔ |
| find wood | ✔ | | | |
| build a fire | ✔ | ✔ | | |
| get water | | ✔ | ✔ | |
| cook dinner | | | | ✔ |

**2.** 1. have to build; don't have to
2. has to find
3. has to get; doesn't have to
4. has to cook; don't have to

**3.** 1. Paula 2. Tina 3. Mike 4. Jeff

## PAGES 38 & 39 Lost at Sea

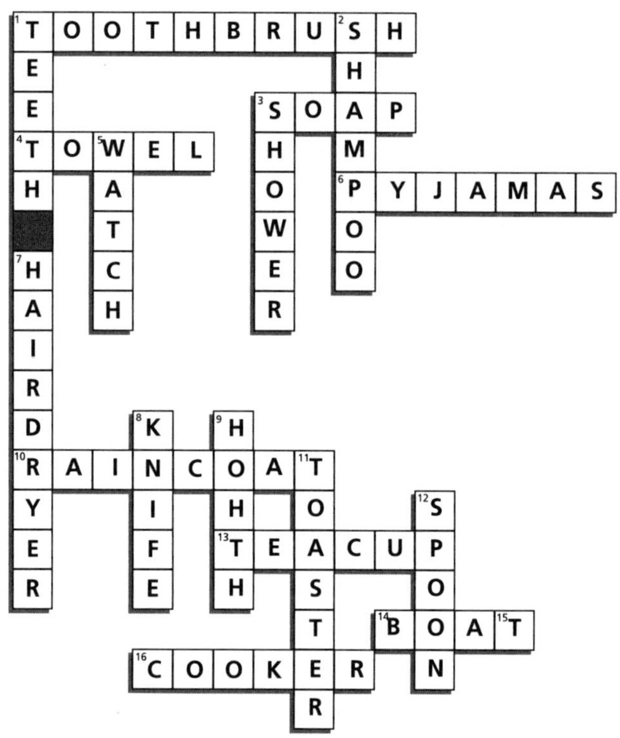

## PAGES 40 & 41 What Should I Do?

**Answers for Problem 1:**

leave the dog outside
tell your friend how to behave with your dog
teach the dog to be good
leave the dog in a room and close the door
give your dog its food when your friend arrives
get a new dog

 

**Answers for Problem 2:**
stay at a friend's house for a week
throw the onions away
soak the onions in water every night – then they won't be as strong
eat the onions and enjoy them!
buy a lot of chewing gum
tell everybody at school that onions are good for you
**Answers for Problem 3:**
ask your aunt about it
talk to your uncle
tell your parents
watch your uncle very carefully
call the police
move to a different bedroom

## PAGES 42 & 43 World of Animals Maze

Sentences 1, 2, 4, 5, 8, 9, 12 are true.
The correct sequence is: 1 → 4 → 7 → 6 → 5→ 3→ 8 → 12 → 2 → 9 → 10 → 11

## PAGES 44 & 45 Snap!

The answers are on the Referee's Answer Key.

## PAGE 46 Birthdays

**DECEMBER**

| Sun | Mon | Tues | Weds | Thurs | Fri | Sat |
|---|---|---|---|---|---|---|
| 1 | 2 | 3 Susan | 4 Katie | 5 David | 6 | 7 Tim |
| 8 Leo | 9 Richard | 10 | 11 Sandra | 12 | 13 | 14 |
| 15 | 16 | 17 Laura | 18 | 19 | 20 John | 21 |
| 22 | 23 | 24 | 25 Fiona | 26 | 27 | 28 |
| 29 | 30 | 31 | | | | |

**JANUARY**

| Sun | Mon | Tues | Weds | Thurs | Fri | Sat |
|---|---|---|---|---|---|---|
| | | | 1 | 2 James | 3 | 4 |

## PAGE 47 What Do You Do...?

**1.** 2. while 3. while 4. when 5. while 6. when
**2.** Students' own answers.

## PAGES 48 & 49 Truth and Lies

2. Has the postman come yet?
No, he hasn't come yet.
3. Has your mum given you any pocket money?
No, not yet. Can I have some?
4. Have you done the washing up yet?
Yes, and I've already put everything away.
5. Has your sister made the breakfast yet?
Yes, we've already eaten it.
6. Have you finished on the phone yet?
Yes, I've already said goodbye.
The true answers are:
2. Yes, he has.
3. Yes, she has.
6. No, I haven't finished yet.

## PAGE 50 Facts and Figures

3. many / 24 hours
4. many / 30 minutes
5. many / 12 months
6. much / 2 litres
7. many / 7 days
8. much / students' own answers
9. many / students' own answers
10. many / 100 cm
11. many / 100 cents
12. much / students' own answers
13. many / 1000 pence
14. much / 1000 g (1 kg)
15. much / 6 litres

## PAGE 51 Who Is The Most Polite?

**1.**
1. Lydia: Can I borrow your camera? Megan: Yes, you can.
2. Tim: Can I open the window, please? Miss Jones: No, you can't.
3. Rich: Give me your camera. Liam: No, ask me politely.

**2.**
1. Tim is the most polite.
2. Rich isn't very polite.

**3.**
1. Can I shut the door, please?
2. Can I borrow some money, please?
3. Can I leave the classroom, please?

## PAGE 52 What Would You Like?

Students' own answers.

## PAGE 53 Class Survey

1. Whose 2. Who 3. Whose 4. Who
5. Who 6. Who 7. Whose 8. Whose

## PAGE 54 Penpals

The following boxes should be ticked:
shopping Saturday
swimming Wednesday

dancing Saturday
ice-skating Tuesday
running –
horse-riding Sunday
walk the dog every day

**PAGE 55 Do You Like ...?**

Students' own answers.

**PAGE 56 Where do people ...?**

**1.** 2. Where do people speak Welsh?
3. Where do people see kangaroos?
4. Where do people play the bagpipes?
5. Where do people visit the pyramids?
6. Where do people celebrate the 4th of July?
7. Where do people dance the flamenco?
8. Where do people grow tea?

**4.**

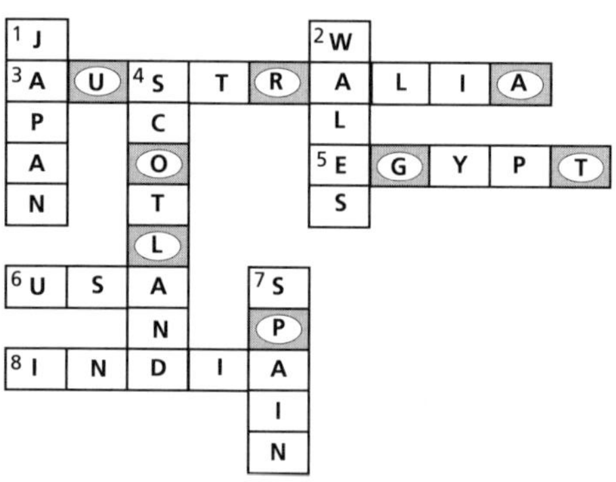

**5.** PORTUGAL

**PAGE 57 A Strange Letter**

You are reading a secret letter. Are you sitting down? Are you eating? Is a teacher watching you? Are you working with a partner? Is your partner learning English? What is your partner wearing? From sun god.

**PAGE 58 Shopping for the Family**

**1.** 3. a 4. a 5. an 6. an 7. a 8. an
9. an 10. a 11. an 12. an 13. a 14. an
15. a

**3.** Mr Gonzalez wants: an umbrella, a dictionary, a tennis racket, an opera ticket and an Underground map.

**PAGE 59 These Aren't My Things**

**1.** 1. This isn't my Walkman, it's hers!
2. This isn't my magazine, it's hers!
3. This isn't my make-up, it's hers!
4. These aren't my rollerskates, they're hers!
5. These aren't my brushes, they're hers!
6. These aren't my teddy bears, they're hers!

**2.** 1. that 2. That 3. those 4. those
5. That 6. That 7. those

**PAGES 60 & 61 A Sleepover**

**1.** Amy is taking: a toothbrush, a tennis racket, a swimming costume and a book. She is also taking some sweets, some keys, some sports clothes, some make-up, and some pyjamas.

**2.** Amy isn't taking any: money, CDs, magazines or homework
Amy isn't taking a: passport or a mobile phone

**3.** B

**PAGE 62 Charlotte's or Charles'?**

1. Victoria's skis 2. has got Peter's tennis racket.
3. has got Tess' riding hat 4. has got Charles' football.
5. has got James' swimming goggles.

**PAGE 63 Christmas Presents**

**1.** Robert – watch, chocolates, car
Ann – books, chocolates; Marie – books, CD player, chocolates; Georgia – books, chocolates; Guy – books, chocolates; Michael – mystery present; Harriet – chocolates

**2.** 1. ours 2. theirs 3. hers 4. mine 5. yours

**PAGES 64 & 65 Word Chain**

**1.** 1. bubble bath 2. doorbell 3. earring
4. go-kart 5. goalpost 6. headphones
7. keyboard 8. light bulb 9. litter bin
10. teacup 11. notebook 12. pencil case
13. schoolbag 14. tennis ball 15. bus stop

**2.**

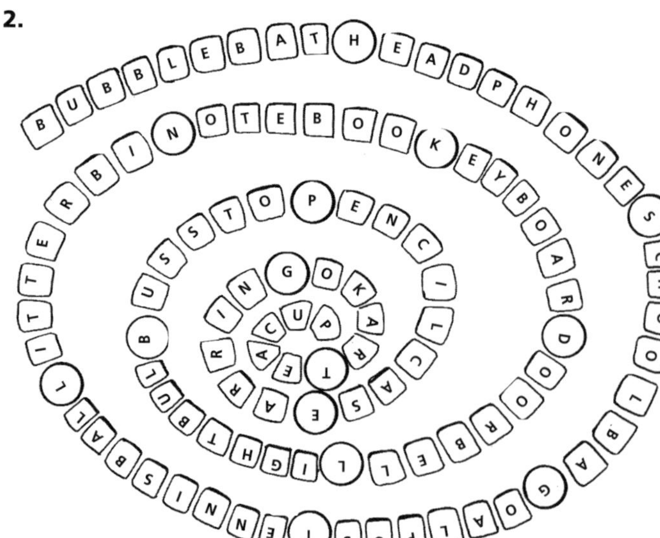

**3.** Some suggested answers: skateboard, hairdryer, dishwasher, video game,babysitter, phone box,daydream etc...

## PAGE 66 Double or Nothing

The answers are on the Referee's Answer Key.

## PAGE 67 Around the World

| | | | | | | | | | | | |
|---|---|---|---|---|---|---|---|---|---|---|---|
| I | R | E | L | A | N | D | O | T | S | U | E |
| T | L | E | M | B | G | E | R | M | A | N | Y |
| A | U | S | T | R | A | L | I | A | P | I | E |
| L | S | H | G | P | U | N | M | K | A | T | R |
| Y | F | C | E | O | B | E | W | A | L | E | S |
| S | C | O | T | L | A | N | D | S | T | D | Y |
| B | C | S | P | A | I | N | N | P | O | S | C |
| E | W | R | O | N | T | S | F | R | A | T | A |
| L | I | T | R | D | K | O | R | E | A | A | N |
| G | J | A | T | H | M | S | A | R | U | T | A |
| I | A | M | U | K | O | R | N | T | N | E | D |
| U | P | E | G | R | E | E | C | E | O | S | A |
| M | A | N | A | T | A | Y | E | G | R | O | I |
| E | N | G | L | A | N | D | D | E | W | F | A |
| C | E | I | S | R | I | K | E | O | A | M | P |
| H | T | H | A | I | L | A | N | D | Y | E | T |
| I | R | U | S | S | I | A | M | Y | E | N | O |

**2.** 2. Spanish 3. Italian 4. French 5. Japanese

## PAGES 68 & 69 California or Florida?

**The following cards are correct:**

Death Valley is drier than the Everglades.

Orlando is hotter than Los Angeles.

An alligator is longer than a hummingbird.

Florida is smaller than California.

California is bigger than Florida.

Disneyland, California, is older than DisneyWorld, Florida.

**The following cards aren't correct:**

Death Valley is wetter than the Everglades.

Orlando is colder than Los Angeles.

An alligator is smaller than a hummingbird.

Florida is bigger than California.

DisneyWorld, Florida, is older than Disneyland, California.

Los Angeles is warmer than Orlando.

## PAGES 70 & 71 Good and Bad Habits

Suggested answers:

| GOOD HABITS: | BAD HABITS: |
|---|---|
| You never tell lies. | You often leave the milk out of the fridge. |
| You always do your homework. | You never eat fresh fruit and vegetables. |
| You usually put away your clothes and tidy your room. | You never clean your shoes. |
| You sometimes help your parents on Saturdays. | You usually play your CDs very loudly. |
| You always wash your hands before you eat. | You often forget your pens and school books. |
| You are always polite to your teachers. | You sometimes write on your desk. |
| You usually wash your face before you go to bed. | |
| You never push other students in the lunch queue. | |
| You always brush your teeth after you eat a meal. | |

## PAGE 72 What Are They Doing?

2. She's sharing her cake generously.
3. She's playing the piano beautifully.
4. He's running quickly.
5. He's shouting angrily.
6. They're laughing happily.
7. It's crying loudly.
8. She's playing badly.

## PAGE 73 Who Lives The Most Dangerously?

Students' own answers.

## PAGES 74 & 75 Put Away the Shopping!

Put the carrots on the bottom shelf, on the right.

Put the butter on the top shelf, on the left

Put the tomatoes on the bottom shelf, in the middle.

Put the chicken on the middle shelf, in the middle.

Put the lettuce on the bottom shelf, on the left.

Put the eggs on the middle shelf, on the right.

Put the yoghurt on the top shelf, on the right.

Put the cheese on the top shelf, in the middle.

Put the sausages on the middle shelf, on the left.

## PAGE 76 A Class Trip

Students' own answers.

**PAGE 77 Put Your Clothes Away!**

**1.** 1. C 2. E 3. F 4. A 5. D 6. B

**2.** 1. Dean 2. Jason 3. Tony
4. Callum 5. Graham 6. Ricky

**3.** taking off; putting on; folding up; folding up; trying on; zipping up; hurry up; put away; take away; put away

**PAGE 78 Give in your homework, please**

| | | | | | | |
|---|---|---|---|---|---|---|
| | | | 1↓ G | | | |
| | | | I | | | |
| | | | V | | | |
| 2↓ P | | 3↓ 4→ T | E | L | L | |
| U | | U | | | | |
| 5→ T | H | R | O | 6↓ W | | |
| | | N | | O | | |
| | | | | 7→ R | U | B |
| | 8↓ 9→ P | I | C | K | | |
| | U | | | | | |
| | 10→ T | U | R | N | | |

**PAGE 79 Help!**

**1.** 1. turn off 2. turn on 3. turn over 4. turn down

**2.** 2. He can't pick up the chair.
3. He can't put on his jumper.
4. He can't tidy up his room. / his toys.

**PAGES 80 & 81 Beach Towel Mystery**

S Eight friends went to the beach.
E They all went swimming in the sea.
A Michelle left her earrings and her watch on her towel.
G When she came back, something was wrong.
U She couldn't find her watch.
L And her earrings were missing, too.
L But there was nobody else on the beach.
S Who stole her things?
The SEAGULLS stole Michelle's things!

**PAGE 82 Friends**

1. I **usually** watch TV in the evening.
2. My **favourite** TV show is *Friends*.
3. My mother **never** watches *Friends*.
4. She doesn't understand why I **always** like to watch it.
5. But perhaps it isn't for **old** women!
6. My mother isn't **very** old, but she isn't young.
7. Perhaps she's **more** intelligent than me!
8. And perhaps I'll listen to her and not watch **so** much TV.
9. But **first**, I've got to watch *Friends*.
10. Oh, no! Mum is watching it **now**!

**PAGE 83 Classrooms**

Suggested answers:
The clock says 10 o'clock in Classroom A, but it says 2 o'clock in Classroom B.
The teacher is a man in Classroom A,
but she is a woman in Classroom B.
They're learning maths in Classroom A,
but they're learning geography in Classroom B.
The bin is full in Classroom A, but it's empty in Classroom B.
The teacher's desk is very messy in Classroom A, but it's tidy in Classroom B.
The calendar says it's October in Classroom A, but it says it's November in Classroom B.
The windows are closed in Classroom A, but they're open in Classroom B.
There are no books on the shelves in Classroom A,
but they're on bookshelves in Classroom B.
There are computers in Classroom A,
but there are dictionaries in Classroom B.

**PAGES 84 & 85 A Seaside Holiday**

Student A:
There are three boys on the beach.
There is a sandcastle.
There are four seagulls in the sky.
There are two umbrellas.
There is one beach ball.
There is one dolphin in the sea.
There is one bucket.
There are three beach towels.
There are four swimmers in the sea.
There are two deckchairs.

Student B:
There are two boys on the beach.
There are two sandcastles.
There are two seagulls in the sky.
There is one umbrella.

 

There are two beach balls.
There are two dolphins in the sea.
There are two buckets.
There are two beach towels.
There are five swimmers in the sea.
There is one deckchair.

**PAGES 86 & 87 What was there ...?**

Suggested answers

Student A:

There were some paintings on the walls yesterday.
There was a TV on the bottom shelf yesterday.
There were some videos on the floor yesterday.
There was a video player on the shelves yesterday.
There was a jacket on the chair yesterday.
There was a stereo system on the floor yesterday.
There were some books on the shelves yesterday.
There weren't any footprints yesterday.
There weren't any gloves yesterday.

Student B:

There aren't any paintings now.
There isn't a TV now.
There aren't any videos now.
There isn't a video player now.
There isn't a jacket now.
There isn't a stereo system now.
There aren't any books now.
There are some footprints on the floor now.
There are some gloves by the window now.

All of our photocopiable resource books are listed below. Free sample pages can be downloaded from the Teacher's section of our website: **www.link2english.com**

**PRIMARY**

Crazy Pictures

Get the Picture

JET Primary Teachers' Resource Book 1

JET Primary Teachers' Resource Book 2

JET Primary Teachers' Resource Book 3

Kids Only Songbook & Cassette 1 (1997/98 – purple)

Kids Only Songbook & Cassette 2 (1998/99 – green)

Kids Only Songbook & Cassette 3 (1999/00 – red)

Kids Only Songbook & Cassette 4 (2000/01 – yellow)

Start With a Song

**SECONDARY**

Timesaver Plays

Timesaver Festivals and Special Days in Britain

Timesaver Holidays and Special Days in the USA

Timesaver Cross-curricular English Activities

Timesaver Grammar Activities (Elementary)

Timesaver Vocabulary Activities (Elementary)

Timesaver Games

New Timesavers

**Material written by:** Coleen Degnan-Veness

**Commissioning Editor:** Emma Grisewood

**Content Editor:** Cheryl Pelteret

**Designer:** Caroline Grimshaw

**Cover photo:** Christopher Woods

**Cover Design:** Kaya Cully

**Illustrations by:** Carl Flint


Printed in the UK by The Baskerville Press Ltd.
Salisbury, Wiltshire